THE END OF MONEY

AND THE STRUGGLE FOR FINANCIAL PRIVACY

BY
RICHARD W. RAHN

THE END OF MONEY
And the Struggle for Financial Privacy

by Richard W. Rahn

Copyright 1999 by Richard W. Rahn

ISBN 0-9638654-2-0

Published in the United States
by Discovery Institute, Seattle, Washington

Printed by Jostens Graphics, North Carolina
Cover design by Robert L. Crowther, II

Books by Discovery fellows, and books published by Discovery Institute Press are available in quantity for promotional and premium use. For information on prices, terms and ordering books contact: Director of Publishing, Discovery Institute, 1402 Third Ave. Suite 400, Seattle, WA 98101 or visit the Discovery website at: www.discovery.org.

To Will and Margie

May the coming digital world bring you liberty and happiness.

ACKNOWLEDGMENTS

The ideas presented in this book developed from extensive discussions and debates I have had with a remarkably diverse and knowledgeable group of individuals over the last two decades. Only a few of those individuals are explicitly noted below, but my sincere thank you also goes to all those present and former colleagues in the Novecon companies, the Cato Institute (which first published my work on digital money and taxation), the Mont Pelerin Society, the American Council for Capital Formation, the Business Leadership Council, the U.S. Chamber of Commerce and the National Chamber Foundation, IRET, Hudson Institute, and Discovery Institute.

I owe a particular debt of gratitude to: my associate, Margaret Rogers, whose facility with English and mathematics helped her turn my rough drafts into a presentable text; and to a great and talented lady, Beverly Danielson, who volunteered many hours and applied her considerable editorial skills to making the book a much better read. My colleague, Bruce MacQueen, contributed his considerable international banking expertise to Chapter 6. Finally, the President of the Discovery Institute, Ambassador Bruce Chapman, lent his sharp pen to the final editing, and gave me a most important bit of advice when I first undertook the project: "Make sure the book is a fast read so it can be managed on a flight from Washington, DC to Seattle."

Additional valuable research and editorial assistance was provided by Taisia Bullard, Margie Parker, Anneli Rahn and Thomas Lent. Rob Crowther and his colleagues at the Discovery Institute get a special thank you for the quality work they have put in on production and marketing.

The following group of economists, bankers, scientific and legal scholars read all or part of the text and made many extensive and helpful comments and suggestions: Norman Bailey, Jim Berson, David Burton, Warren Coats, Michel Derobert, George Gilder, Juhani Heinonen, Gina Knight, Henry Manne, Don Schwarzkopf, Howard Segermark, Beryl Sprinkel, David Thompson, Peter Wallison, and John Yoder.

A decade ago we formed a small group of thinkers to explore the possibility of making the ideas that the Nobel Prize winning economist and philosopher, F. A. Hayek, and others had presented concerning the denationalization of currency a practical reality. The technology was not available at that time to make non-governmental money feasible, but that discussion group served to stimulate my thoughts on the future of money and financial privacy. In addition to several of those mentioned above, members of the group included Ed Crane, Larry Hunter, Paul Craig Roberts, and Ron Utt, all of whom have continued to be of assistance, and my late colleagues Allen Abrahams and Bob Krieble.

Finally, the author alone takes responsibility for the content of this book.

TABLE OF CONTENTS

PREFACE

Money—as we know it—is coming to an end. Even now, government-produced paper and coin "money" is becoming less important and, within the next two decades, will almost entirely disappear.

Webster's dictionary defines money as "any circulating medium of exchange, including coins, paper money, and demand deposits." *Money will disappear because a circulating medium of exchange is needed only when a time interval is required between the liquidation of an earning or useful asset and the acquisition of a new asset or service. In the digital age, such time intervals are no longer needed, hence there is no need for traditional money.*

Technologies that have resulted from the invention of the microchip and digital electronics are about to alter how the economic world works in very fundamental ways and, in turn, how governments function. These new technologies, including the Internet, personal computers, "smart cards" and "smart devices," and easily usable encryption, will accelerate growth in real incomes for most people and increase personal freedom. How quickly and fully people participate in the full benefits of the "digital age" will depend in large measure on how quickly and fully governments adapt, in a constructive manner, to the new technological reality.

Governments can hinder the process by trying to restrict financial privacy, the use of the Internet, smart cards, free trade, and free banking. They can refuse to reduce high tax rates, and in particular taxes on capital; and they can resist reductions in government regulations and spending. But those governments that hinder the process will cause their citizens to fall behind in the race for increased prosperity and freedom. On the other hand, those governments that quickly adjust their laws, regulations, and practices in order to embrace the new technologies will bring joy and prosperity to their citizens. Governments have a long history of attempting to ban or restrict new technologies, including attempts to prohibit the use of the new inventions of the automobile and vaccinations. But they almost never prevail.

The international monetary chaos that began in Southeast Asia in mid-1997, and spread across much of the rest of the world in 1998, reminded us once again that the best of the world's central bankers can neither predict with great accuracy nor control relative monetary flows and values. The next shock to the world's financial markets could result from the year 2000 computer problem and the inability of governments to manage either the preparations or the consequences adequately. As non-governmental digital money grows, individuals will be able to protect themselves from the mistakes of central bankers and misguided politicians. Individuals and businesses will make some mistakes, but these individual errors will not have the same far-reaching negative effects on innocent players in the marketplace that the errors of the government bankers and politicians now do.

This book is intended to give readers an understanding of how the world of digital electronics will alter the economic and political world. It will also provide a road map for government officials and other policy-makers to ensure that their citizens can take full and speedy advantage of the new opportunities. Finally, the book will be a warning to those policy-makers and bureaucrats who may be inclined to resist the inevitable change. It will explain why this opposition will ultimately fail, though it may well cause misery in the meantime.

The chief advantage of change is the clear economic lesson of freedom. It is no coincidence that the economically freest countries on earth are also the most prosperous. In the future, the relationship between economic freedom and prosperity will become even more apparent.

The economically freest countries and political entities—Switzerland, the US, Hong Kong, and New Zealand—have achieved far more success than the less free. For example, the US and Switzerland have the highest real per capita wages and also the lowest rates of unemployment of the world's countries. They both have very low tariffs. Obviously, wage rates and job opportunities have not been destroyed by competition from low-wage countries, as protectionists would argue. Successful countries all have relatively small government sectors and far less economic and financial regulation than other countries.

The digital world will force change toward smaller, less intrusive, and less centralized government everywhere. In the "digital age," opportunity and greatest rewards will go to the citizens whose governments have freer tax, spending and economic regulatory systems—systems such as those of Hong Kong (before the takeover by the People's Republic of China).

The conclusions in this book are not based upon a particular ideology, but upon the empirical evidence of what works and what does not, and where the new technologies appear to be taking us. Neither traditional conservatives nor liberals are likely to be totally comfortable with the operation of the world economy in the digital age. Politicians of both the left and right will lose power to non-political market forces, and the loss of power will cause considerable angst. Change may be upsetting but it is inevitable, and fortunately most often for the good.

Chapter I

OVERVIEW OF THE STRUGGLE FOR FINANCIAL PRIVACY AND FREEDOM

*The natural progress of things is for liberty to yield
and governments to gain ground.*

—Thomas Jefferson

As you read these words, there is an almost unknown but intense global struggle occurring. Its outcome will likely affect the freedom and economic well-being of every man, woman, and child on the planet.

This struggle, simply put, is between those who see in new technologies the potential for individuals to achieve unparalleled financial freedom and economic growth, and those who view all new innovations as suspect and a threat to law enforcement and national defense. The new technologies that together are enabling the world's people to escape the financial tyranny of the state are: the Internet; PC's with modems; "smart cards"; and readily available, easy-to-use, and—for all practical purposes—unbreakable, public key and private key encryption. These technologies are in the process of coming together in a way that will enable people to move their money and financial assets to almost any point on the globe, at close to the speed of light, without the knowledge of any government.

Government bureaucrats who understand the ramifications of what is now beginning to happen fear for their own existence. Government's near-monopoly on money is about to end. Involuntary taxation of financial capital will be a relic of the past. Traditional methods of detecting and monitoring the financial activities of tax cheats, drug dealers, money launderers, and terrorists, as well as political opponents and enemies, is about to end.

The state already has lost the technological battle. The question now is whether the state will face this technological reality and redesign its tax and financial systems, as well as anti-crime practices, to allow people to do what they will do, in a lawful manner. If the statist bureaucrats refuse to adapt, they can continue to fight the new technologies through attempts to further increase government intrusion into and control over the lives of citizens. Those citizens who abide by the laws shall then be monitored in all of their daily routines, while those willing to commit criminal acts will foil the monitoring systems, and will find ways to operate undetected. If extensive monitoring occurs, it will result in a citizenry further alienated from and hostile to a government that becomes more oppressive. Such governments are doomed. This book is a plea to avoid such an outcome. Rational people can develop appropriate means to provide the necessary revenues for legitimate activities of the state, including crime prevention, without trampling on civil liberties or banning beneficial new technologies.

Today, there are more than 3,000 Federal criminal offenses in the US, plus millions of regulations. The Internal Revenue Code alone reaches more than 9,000 pages. Obviously, no human can come close to knowing all of the regulations that government requires him or her to follow. The result is that virtually everyone at some time or another violates some law or regulation of which he had no knowledge. Such a citizen can be indicted and convicted at any time for some violation of law. Of course, the state cannot possibly catch everyone, so it engages in selective prosecution. If someone becomes unpopular with a powerful faction within the political establishment for some reason or another—say a Michael Milken or a Leona Helmsley—he can be investigated until some rule he has broken is found, and then he can be prosecuted on those charges.

The expansion of regulations on political conduct, for example, has gone so far that nearly any public leader or his campaign can be shown to have violated some legal requirement. This makes him liable to official or media investigations any time it is politically convenient. If he attempts to deflect the attack, his interpretation of his actions can be termed a cover-up, perjury or obstruction of justice. Even if he battles the charge and wins, he loses precious time and money. Sometimes the "crime" is nothing more than an attempt to hide an embarrassment that is not a real crime, such as former Housing Secretary Henry Cisneros' lie to the FBI about his payments to a former mistress.

Given that many in the Washington establishment—both members of Congress and the Administration—have done far worse, it was hypocritical to single out Mr. Cisneros. Virtually no one is immune to this process, and the result is that we increasingly become a government of men rather than laws.

The current battles are a part of the long struggle between those of more libertarian leanings and those of more statist leanings (or, between the classical liberals and socialists in the European sense). In this long struggle, most of the battles have resulted in some sort of muddled accommodation of the other side. What makes this current war different is that there is little room for muddled accommodation. The state will know everything or it will know little or nothing. The new electronic technologies enable information to flow through a variety of media, from anywhere, to anyone, at any time.

The challenge that we face as citizens of the world will be to recognize the burgeoning technologies before us as tools, and to understand that it is in our interest to integrate into our lives and society the opportunity to use such tools in ways that will not violate our liberty.

The World Ahead

The nine most terrifying words in the English language are:
'I'm from the government and I'm here to help.'

— Ronald Reagan

In the digital age, the government can attempt to have a detailed record of our every financial transaction and of our complete financial status, or it can accept the reality that it will know only what we want it to know.

Government officials around the world have provided a number of rationalizations to justify their intrusions into the financial privacy of citizens. These rationalizations can be put into two broad categories:

1. The need to obtain private financial information in order to ensure payment of all taxes due;

2. The need for law-enforcement agencies to have access to private financial information in order to detect and prosecute drug dealers, terrorists, spies, kidnappers, money launderers, and other assorted reprehensible folks.

In addition, governments have found a profitable side business of selling data about their citizens—such as information about their automobiles and driving practices—to commercial companies. These companies in turn sell the data as market intelligence and research to vendors of goods and services.

Under totalitarian regimes, free speech and a free press are prohibited. Those who write and speak about things the state does not like are branded as criminals, and punished. As technology changes, however, it becomes increasingly difficult for state authorities to regulate what is published and what the people hear.

Economic development has come to depend on the wide dissemination of information. The tools of dissemination—the printed word, radio and TV, telephones, movies, and most recently the Internet—have become cheaper and cheaper, and therefore far more available, leaving residual totalitarian regimes in a dilemma. They need to allow their populations to have access to the information-dissemination tools if their economies are going to improve, but these same tools can be used to receive and transmit politically prohibited ideas.

If people have PC's with printers and modems, copying machines, telephones, radios and TV's, how can anyone long prevent them from using these devices for non-approved political communication? The short answer is that no one can.

The rulers of the Soviet Union found that they could not

prevent ideas about freedom and democracy from getting to the masses, because the new technologies overwhelmed the state apparatus to control information. The lesson of the hopeless battle to control information was learned well by the leaders of the new Russia. Despite all of the current turmoil, Russia now has a free and open press, and virtually every faction of political opinion has its vehicles of dissemination.

The rulers of the People's Republic of China are now going through this same losing struggle to control information and still create a modern society. Currently, they are trying to control the information that is transmitted and received over the Internet. They know that they need the Internet to stay competitive, but they have yet to admit or understand that a society cannot get full value from this technology unless a substantial segment of the population can access the information that is on the global net. Full access and political control are so contradictory that it is only a matter of time before the Chinese, like the old Soviets, give up trying to control information.

What the advocates of limitations on financial privacy in the United States have yet to understand or acknowledge is that they are in the same position as the censors in the old Soviet regime and in China today. They are fighting a battle they cannot win. They can only brand as criminals those who refuse to follow their unenforceable restrictions. Yes, they will find and prosecute some number of miscreants, much as the KGB punished those caught listening to Radio Free Europe, or using the Xerox for an unapproved purpose. But many of those who choose freedom and privacy will not be deterred.

America had its experiment with Prohibition in the 1920s. The production and domestic sale of alcohol was made illegal, and the advocates of Prohibition had many good reasons for their stance. However, many Americans did not believe that the government should prohibit them from getting a drink, and they were not about to submit. The technology of how to make beer, wine, and whiskey was too well known. The law was unenforceable. Instead, Prohibition resulted in a big rise in serious crime, particularly organized crime, and a diminished respect for government. The war on the bootleggers was an unwinnable war and the crime fighters, in their desperation, often trampled over fundamental civil liberties. Prohibition was repealed in 1933, but the organized crime that it had spurred did not evaporate, and significant damage was done to society. Chicago, the city of Al Capone, provided one of the most well-known examples of the rise of organized crime:

> By 1927, Al Capone controlled not only all illicit commerce in Illinois—from alcohol to gambling to prostitution— but also the majority of the politicians, including most police commissioners, the mayor of Chicago, and the governor. By the end of the decade, organized crime was so organized they had a national convention in Atlantic City. . . . Even when the chairman of the board, Mr. Capone, took an enforced vacation in 1931 and Prohibition ended in 1933, the "company" did not go out of business. It simply found new merchandise and services to market.[1]

Evading the government restrictions on financial privacy will be much easier than making gin in the bathtub. The only result from the restrictions will be an enlargement of the government as it hires more "crime fighters" to get normally law-abiding citizens to "come clean" with the most intimate details of their financial lives. As these crime fighters struggle with this impossible task, more civil liberties will wither, and

---

[1]Peter McWilliams, Ain't Nobody's Business If You Do: The Absurdity of Consensual Crimes in a Free Society (Los Angeles: Prelude Press, 1993), 71.

ordinary citizens will have an increasing disdain for government.

Advocating the abolition of laws and regulations that restrict financial privacy is not the same as condoning terrorism,
drug dealing, or tax evasion. It is merely acknowledging that
the new technology has made it impossible, at least in any
reasonably cost-effective manner, to enforce such laws and
restrictions and at the same time preserve civil liberties. Because we still mostly protect freedom of speech and freedom
of the press, the life of law-enforcement agencies is far more
difficult. But most people realize that to retain some mod-
icum of freedom for the people, there have to be restrictions
on what law-enforcement and tax-collection agencies are allowed to do.

The American founders explicitly understood that the
great danger to the liberties of the people was unchecked
government. They recognized that it is far better that ten guilty
men go free, than one innocent man be punished.

Those who have the romantic idea that government is
nearly always good and benign might reflect on the twentieth
century, in which totalitarian governments have killed well
over a hundred million people. Even though there are no
good figures on the total number of people killed worldwide
by assorted drug dealers and Mafia gangs in this century, it is
probably well under a hundred thousand people. That is a
terrible toll of human tragedy, but minor compared to the
transgressions of assorted brutes acting with the force of the
state.

Our founding fathers, being students of John Locke, believed that the primary function of government was to protect
person and property. Government should be used to preserve
life, not to destroy it. The digital age gives citizens the power

to keep governments in check by immediately disclosing abuses to millions of people. With today's technology, it would have been hard for Hitler and Stalin to keep their concentration camps off the world's TV screens. If both the media and financial sector can be kept largely free of government control, such atrocities as the organized, systematic killing machines that operated over a course of several years in the mid-twentieth century might well be prevented from ever occurring again.

Americans, particularly, are often attached to the notion that evils only occur in non-democratic regimes. Fortunately, for the most part this is true—but not true enough. Even in America, the toll of government abuse of its own citizens during this century is mind-boggling. It was the US government, in World War II, that put totally innocent American citizens in internment camps and seized their property without due process of law, merely because they happened to be of Japanese ancestry. This same government enforced segregation and the Jim Crow laws. Unfortunately, these are only examples selected from a long list. Reprehensible behavior on the part of officials of the US government continues. Who can forget that it was officials of the US Treasury and Justice Departments that killed innocent American children at Waco, Texas and Ruby Ridge, Idaho? Who has been sent to jail for these crimes, or the abuses at the IRS?—No one.

Given such a history, there is little reason to believe that the same people that have had the responsibility for the oversight of the IRS and the FBI will not abuse their knowledge of the most intimate details of your financial life. In any society, there are always some who take advantage of the information, authority, or power with which they have been entrusted.

Most people working for the government are honest and

try to do a good job, and America has greatly benefited from its responsible civil servants. The problem is that a small number of irresponsible people with considerable power can do great damage. What matters, therefore, are the constraints under which they operate.

Privacy: To Be Let Alone

A major focus of this book is on actual and potential abuse of financial information by governments, because that is one of the greatest dangers to the liberty of the people. This focus is not intended to obscure the very real problem of invasions and misuse of financial privacy by businesses and individuals, nor invasions of privacy in general.

Privacy is a precious commodity. People should be able to live their lives largely as they see fit, provided that they do not impinge on the rights of others. As Justice Louis Brandeis said, the makers of the Constitution "conferred, as against the government, the right to be let alone—the most comprehensive of rights and the right most valued by civilized men."

The right to be let alone can conflict with other rights, most notably freedom of the press. Does the press have the right to run pictures of you in the newspaper if you are not voluntarily involved in some public controversy or explicitly seeking press attention for some cause or commercial endeavor? The answer is normally yes. How about nude photographs taken by the paparazzi using powerful telephoto lenses, as happened to Jacqueline Kennedy Onassis during an outing to a private beach? The excuse for publishing those was that she was a public person. But if you are not a public person, does the press have the right to take and publish such pictures? Should there have been more limits on the photographers who constantly followed Princess Diana? These are only some of the questions that arise when we try to understand the conflicts around our concepts of privacy.

When people lived in small nomadic or agricultural groups, there was little in the way of privacy among members of the group. They worked, played, and slept together for protection. They had little in the way of singularly independent lives, and hence little privacy from the group. On the other hand, they had a great deal of privacy from the population at large. Given very limited travel and virtually no mass communication beyond the range of a single human voice, small groups had extensive privacy from each other, even though they might have lived only a few miles apart. The diversity in actions, practices, and beliefs of these small groups of humans occurred because of the "privacy" that they had from other groups. (Without these distinct religious, gastronomic, and sexual practice differences among small associations of humans, the anthropologists of today would have little to study.)

Individuals only began to have some of our modern concepts of privacy upon the growth of urban centers. The growth of cities, which allowed people to have anonymity from others, but still interact with them on a frequent basis, is only a phenomenon of the past few thousand years. Individuals or small bodies of people could engage in discussions or actions unbeknownst to their fellow citizens of the city or large town. The assemblage of small private groups in urban settings gave rise to some of the most notable political changes that mankind has experienced. These changes have been both constructive, such as those brought about by America's founding fathers—and destructive, such as the changes unleashed by Lenin's Bolsheviks. The technology of intrusion available to either King George III or Czar Nicholas II was insufficient to allow them to know what the enemies of their regimes were planning.

Up to this century, plotters for and against tyranny alike did worry about traitors in their midst and about careless conversations being overheard, or perhaps their writings being stolen. However, if precautions were taken, these dangers could be minimized, for governments' monitoring capabilities had not significantly improved since the invention of the state. The first wiretaps were invented shortly after the invention of the telegraph 150 years ago. But only in the aftermath of World War I were secret microphones and secret cameras, as well as the science of decryption, developed. George Orwell's novel <u>1984</u>, published in 1948, depicted a coming age in which the state controlled and abused these technologies, and provided a nightmare vision that scared and alerted the world.

Fortunately, technology has developed in such a way that it is not only of great use to the state, but also to the individual who wishes to protect himself or herself from predatory states or individuals.

Video technology has developed to the point where individuals can be spotted from space, or in a room by a camera with a lens smaller than an eraser on a pencil. Police departments in many cities around the world put up surveillance cameras in high crime areas or busy places. Private companies use surveillance cameras to protect their property and monitor their employees, vendors, and customers for efficiency and safety. Microphones have evolved to the point where they can pick up conversations from great distances, and have been miniaturized to the point where they are no bigger than a microchip and are thus almost invisible. It is now nearly impossible for a person to say with certainty that he is neither being photographed nor listened to at any time or in any place.

The only form of communication remaining that an individual, with a high degree of certainty, can know is not being monitored is highly encrypted digital data. Other than a gun, this is one of the last individual defenses against corrupt or totalitarian institutions and individuals. And this is why it must be preserved for the ordinary citizen.

In a world where computers can store enormous quantities of information about anybody, it becomes increasingly important for the individual to have knowledge about what is being stored concerning himself or herself, its accuracy, and who has access to it. On a daily basis, the media report about people who have been severely damaged, financially and otherwise, by those who have incorrectly reported information about them or misused such information. For example, the Washington Post reported an instance in which a woman had lost three jobs as a result of inaccurate information compiled in a database.

> [The woman's] name, date of birth and Social Security number inexplicably popped up in a Baltimore County computer in connection with four child protective services cases from 1987 to 1996. The database includes witnesses, victims and suspects, but [the woman] never lived or worked in Baltimore County, and an official there later blamed her inclusion on a data entry error.[2]

By the time the mistake was sorted out, the woman had lost her job as a child care director. Later, she faced more problems as a result of other errors in the criminal record databases, and missed other jobs, even though it was widely acknowledged that she had done nothing wrong. These types of reporting mistakes can occur in all kinds of databases, jeopardizing not only careers, but also reputations and credit ratings.

[2]Eugene Meyer, "Md. Woman Caught in Wrong Net," Washington Post 15 December 1997, C1.

Most people do not want to have total privacy about their financial affairs because without some disclosure, it becomes almost impossible to obtain credit. There is no right to credit; it is a privilege. To obtain it, you need to convince someone that you will have both the means and the honest intention to pay back the money that is lent to you. Usually the reason that people are unable to obtain credit is because they have a poor history of repayment or no credit history at all. Young people frequently are unable to get credit because they have no payment history, a "Catch 22." Many of us were taught to borrow some money or apply for a credit card, even if we did not need it at the time, in order to establish a payment history—which is still good advice. Indeed, in our current economy, those who think that they have no need for credit find that it is difficult to rent a car or make a hotel or airline reservation without a credit card.

But while most people voluntarily give up some financial privacy in order to obtain credit, this voluntary act should not imply that their rights to privacy about anything other than what they have freely chosen to disclose should be abridged. As debit cards and smart cards become more widespread, this problem should be partially remedied. The fact remains, those who choose not to use some form of bank card will find it difficult to make certain types of purchases.

Businesses have an interest in knowing the buying habits of customers, as well as their credit ratings. This legitimate commercial need has spawned a huge data collection business. Data collection companies acquire records of virtually any purchase you make with a check, debit or credit card. Magazine publishers sell their subscription lists, a practice that has now spread to most other forms of commerce where potential customer lists are useful. For example, if you make a purchase at your local garden shop, you can almost be assured that the shop will sell your name and address to the seed catalog companies.

Much of this is to the consumer's advantage, because it enables vendors to target their promotions to customers with particular interests. That in turn makes it easier for those with particular interests to obtain information about products they may wish to purchase, because the vendors know who is likely to want to receive specific product information. You can be assured that information about your purchase will not be recorded and sold only if you pay in cash and provide no personal information to the seller.

Even though most purchase and credit reporting is inoffensive or even desirable, abuses take place. We are all bombarded by targeted telephone solicitations. In far worse cases of abuse, identities are stolen, and incorrect information gets into data banks, which can do great harm. The Chicago Tribune reported a kind of fraud that is growing rapidly:

> A caller from a ritzy department store wanted to know when he [Joe W. Woods] would pay the bill for silk sheets and women's cologne.
> Trouble was, one, Joe W. Woods didn't have an account at Lord & Taylor, and, two, he didn't buy any such items.
> "I don't know your company," Woods told the caller. "You have something wrong."
> The department store employee was not amused. She rattled off his Social Security number and a list of other accounts on his credit report, among them: Saks Fifth Avenue, Radio Shack, Neiman Marcus. None of them were accounts Woods had opened.
> "My temperature went up 20 degrees,"

Woods remembered, "and I said, 'I'm in big trouble.'"

Someone had ripped off his identity.[3]

Most misinformation on individuals and businesses is a result of incompetence somewhere in the data collection and reporting chain, but the harm often can be as great as false reports due to malice. It is easy to find services over the Internet and elsewhere that will dig up information on people for both good and bad reasons. The problem is that there is no standard for accuracy for the information that is reported. People can be denied credit because of false credit reports, or denied jobs because of false arrest or conviction reports.

The Internet also is becoming important as a sales channel for goods and services. These transactions, like those over the telephone, are subject to fraud and theft. Credit card and debit card numbers can be and are stolen. Fortunately, a number of innovative solutions have been developed. Various sorts of digital money, such as DigiCash and CyberCash[4], have been created, and easy-to-use encryption is now available to protect credit card and debit card transactions.

The computer has enabled the creation of massive information data banks about all aspects of individuals' lives. Medical records are some of the most sensitive, because most people value the privacy of their medical condition and treatment. According to Money Magazine, "The private Medical Information Bureau (MIB) houses files on some 15 million Americans, which are used by MIB's member insurance companies to help determine who gets life and health insurance and what they'll pay. Medical personnel in managed-care networks can read your files that aren't kept at MIB too. So

---

[3]Annette Kondo, "Nothing Personal: To Avoid Fraud, Guard Identity Data With Care," Chicago Tribune, 20 October 1995.

[4]More about these payment systems can be found at their respective websites, http://www.digicash.com and http://www.cybercash.com

can pharmacy benefits-management companies and some employers."[5] One does not need much imagination to envision how such information can be abused, or how incorrect data can cause great hardship.

Horror stories also abound about unethical businesses invading children's privacy or the legitimate privacy needs of the businesses' own workers. Fortunately, in democratic states most of these private sector abuses can be dealt with by appropriate legislation, regulation, and law enforcement—or just plain exposure. There is nothing like the spotlight of attention on inappropriate business behavior to bring about swift change. Over time the market does work—though not always perfectly—and long-term abuses of worker and consumer trust are exceedingly rare unless government grants a business some sort of monopoly right.

The reason that free-market democracy largely has triumphed around the globe is that, despite its imperfections, it works far better than any alternative economic system. More people benefit in more ways, and fewer are abused under free-market democratic capitalism. When government allows it to properly function, capitalism delivers both the goods and liberty. The same cannot be said of activities managed by government. Over time, governments tend to devolve into inefficient bureaucratic tyrannies.

Given that the greatest threat to our future prosperity and liberty comes not from business and the private sector, but from government, this book will focus on the struggle and need for financial freedom. The world's people will be neither truly prosperous nor free unless governments retreat from their seemingly never-ending desire to control the production and use of money.

---

[5]James E. Reynolds, "Protect Your Privacy: Medical Privacy," Money Online.

Digital electronic technology enables people to do for themselves what governments attempted to do in the past. The computer, global communications, and the Internet are destroying governments' monopolies on information and money. A person with an inexpensive device to access the Internet can learn practically anything that is known by just about anyone. Almost any individual or institution that has an asset that can be securitized will soon be able to create financial instruments that can provide most of the functions of money.

A major and growing portion of foreign trade is in ser-vices—financial services (such as banking and insurance), busi-ness services, engineering and architectural services, legal ser-vices, etc. Many of these services can be provided over the Internet, and hence the providers can be located almost anywhere in the world. Many service providers can easily move their places of business to jurisdictions that have a favorable tax and regulatory environment. Free trade in services increasingly will become a necessity, because govern-ments will find they can neither regulate nor tax such transac-tions, because consumers will receive much of the "product" by way of the Internet in digitally encrypted form. Govern-ments that fail to move to free trade in services will find they are faced with the digital equivalent of trying to sweep back the sea.

Any country with a tax code that has high marginal tax rates on labor and capital, particularly financial capital, will see its tax base shrink, as people increasingly seek and acquire goods and services abroad and invest in low-tax jurisdictions through the Internet. For instance, if you wish to hire someone to write computer software, you may consider competent professionals anywhere in the world, because you can obtain the work output over the Internet as well as provide instructions and make payments. Professionals living in high-tax jurisdictions either will have to reduce their hourly wages or forgo the opportunity for the work. Purchasers of software are interested in getting the best product for the lowest delivered after-tax price. Many professional software writers may choose not to pay income taxes to their governments when their client is in a foreign country.

Tax evasion will be easier since they will be able to send their product over the Internet in encrypted fashion, and hence the government will not know of the untaxed export, and the seller can instruct the purchaser to make payment to the seller's account in a no-tax jurisdiction.

Holders of financial capital (*i.e.*, stocks and bonds, currency, gold, etc.) also will find it increasingly easy to move their portfolios to low-tax jurisdictions. Again, they will do this in an encrypted format so that their own government will not know where it has ultimately gone. When tax evasion becomes this easy, like the purchase of whiskey in a '20s speakeasy, many currently law-abiding citizens will find the temptation too great to resist.

The correct response from governments to these new temptations will be to redesign their tax systems. High marginal-rate tax systems are destructive to economic growth to begin with, and they do not maximize tax revenue. The taxation of capital is particularly destructive, because it has the same effect as eating your own "seed corn." Most capital has been taxed at least once—when it was first earned—if not again thereafter. Taxation of capital reduces the amount that is available for new investment, yet capital is what increases productivity and creates new jobs. So, the fact that people will have the ability to avoid destructive taxation is a net plus to economic growth, opportunity, and freedom.

Governments that do not modify their tax systems, but try

to respond to the new technologies by so-called tougher enforcement, will succeed only in criminalizing the actions of a much larger portion of their populations, while at the same time reducing economic growth and freedom.

Benign governments will face the digital age by legalizing financial privacy, redesigning their tax systems, and shrinking their own economic and social roles. Oppressive governments will face the digital age by attempting to abolish financial privacy, and then drown in a sea of corruption and disrespect. The following presents the case for legal financial privacy, and explains the necessity of changing our tax laws, and our trade and financial laws, to deal with the reality of the digital world.

Chapter II

MONEY IN THE DIGITAL AGE

P eople do not want money—what they want is the ability to acquire goods and services. Money is only useful as a means to facilitate trade. Fortunately, new technologies will enable people to acquire the goods they want without holding or handling cash, which is a troublesome, non-earning asset. In the future, trade will be executed by instantaneous and simultaneous debiting and crediting liquid wealth accounts, held by both banking and non-banking institutions. The new electronic digital payments technology will enable property rights claims on real assets, such as stock and bond funds, or gold, to be utilized as the medium of exchange for virtually all transactions. In sum, when businesses or individuals wish to purchase a good or service, they will provide an electronic instruction—directly or indirectly—to their bank or other financial intermediary. The instruction will state that an amount equal to the nominal value of the purchase should be transferred immediately (with no time lag) to the account of the seller of the good or service. As a result, there will be no loss of interest earned, nor will there be any need for a traditional wholesale interbank clearing system. The buyer and seller will have transferred wealth almost instantaneously and without risk of non-payment. By avoiding the use of government-produced fiat money, with all of its uncertainty and instability, some of the curse of inflation and payments insecurity that plague the world will disappear.

The following is a simplified explanation of the mechanics of the monetary revolution now upon us. It is intended to provide a basic understanding of the coming world in a manner that can be understood by anyone, including those who are not formally schooled in economics. (Readers desiring a more detailed explanation of the mechanics, concepts, and issues raised in this section should read the explanatory footnotes, and refer to the bibliography).

The Evolution of Money

If Karl, instead of writing a lot about Capital,
made a lot of Capital, it would have been much better.

— Karl Marx's mother (probably apocryphal)

What most people think of as money—the paper currency and coins in their purses or wallets, and the bank account against which they write checks—will gradually disappear over the next couple of decades.[6]

---

[6]There are now several types of payment systems, and some of the new ones are gaining popularity. Cash, bank deposits, debit cards, checks, payment orders, travelers checks, digital cash, electronic purses, and stored value cards are all means of payment, but some are money and others are instruments (contracts, technologies, instructions) for transferring ownership of money. The paper currency and coins that we think of as money, and checks, are more cumbersome and less efficient than the new types of payment, such as digital cash. Digital cash is basically an encoded message that gives the owner of the message a claim on the issuer. The amount of digital cash in circulation would be measured by banks' or other issuers' abilities to redeem it. (From the draft paper by Warren Coats and Charles Kelly, August 1996, "The Simple Analytics of Digital Money: Finance in Cyberspace," International Monetary Fund).

Conventional money will disappear because it is costly and cumbersome. Paper currency and coins can easily be lost or stolen. Conventional money is also bulky to transport and time-consuming to use in business transactions. It requires merchants to keep a monetary "inventory" in order to make change. (When used to buy merchandise from machines, such as a soda vending machine, costly coin and bill handling mechanisms must be installed. These mechanisms are subject to frequent mechanical breakdown and theft from both employees and outsiders). All of this "inventory" of currency and coins is at risk and does not earn its owners any return.

Money is also costly to print or mint. According to the United States Mint's Office of Public Affairs, 20.2 billion coins were minted in FY 1996, at a total cost of $352 million. The Office of Printing and Engraving states that 9.4 billion notes were printed in FY 1996, at a cost of 4.1¢ per note, for a total cost of $385.4 million. All together, this means that the United States spent $737.7 million in FY 1996 to produce the 1996 issuance of currency.

Paper currency is subject to counterfeiting. As copying technology has become more advanced, counterfeiting has become easier. Bank note printing companies have responded by developing very sophisticated paper currency containing embedded images and metallic threads to thwart the counterfeiters. Despite these advances, technology-proficient counterfeit operators continue to find ways to develop passable currency. It is claimed that groups in Iran are already able to produce passable likenesses of the new US $100 bill, and that they are supplying substantial amounts of counterfeit US currency to the former Soviet Union and Eastern Europe.

Bank checking accounts are also cumbersome and time-consuming to use. Think how annoying it is to waste time

standing in a line at the supermarket while people write out
checks, and the time you have to spend paying your monthly
bills. Checks are subject to considerable error because of
mistakes people make in writing them and the fact that much
handwriting is almost illegible. Clerks at banks have to copy
and translate these personal scrawls into machine-readable
language, and the checks have to be physically transported to
clearing centers and ultimately back to the check writers for
reconciling their accounts. On average, it costs the US banking system approximately $1.50 to process each check. An
estimated total of 65 billion checks were processed in 1996,
for a total cost of $97.5 billion. That was more than the total
profits of the entire US banking system.[7]

Electronic payments, whether made with smart cards, debit
cards, credit cards, or made directly from computer to computer, eliminate most of these problems and greatly reduce
costs. An electronic payment, by being virtually instantaneous,
also eliminates the distinction between credit and debit transfers.

Again, it is not money that people desire, but the functions
of money. Money is supposed to be a medium and unit of
account, a store of value, a medium of exchange, and a
medium of settlement.[8] It arose as a mechanism to facilitate

[7]These estimates are courtesy of the research department of the American Bankers Association.
[8]Because of the variety of meanings of the word "money" and its many functions, we will
include the following definitions in the interest of clarity. We shall conform to these definitions,
taken from Explorations in the New Monetary Economics, by Tyler Cowen and Randall Kroszner,
pages 9 - 11, throughout this book.
A *store of value* is a durable asset or commodity which serves as an intertemporal abode of
purchasing power. Many assets serve as stores of value; the store of value function is not uniquely
associated with "money."
A *medium of exchange* is an asset or commodity which is held for purposes of indirect
exchange and can be transferred to make purchases and retire debts. Creditors and traders are
willing to accept exchange media to satisfy debt obligations or in compensation for the purchase of
commodities. Use of a medium of exchange also may trigger a transfer of settlement media. Media
of exchange need not have a physical embodiment but can exist in the form of bookkeeping entries,
similar to today's US Treasury securities.
Whether an asset is a medium of exchange is a matter of context and degree. Merchants and

the exchange of goods and services because simple barter was too inefficient. Before the development of money, a farmer who had a surplus of wheat and a farmer who had a surplus of cows could arrange an exchange of wheat for cows where they would both be better off. There were problems with the barter system, of course. In the case just mentioned, for example, the smallest unit that could be traded was one cow, and both the cow and the wheat were perishable over time.

To solve these problems, early man developed money. Early money consisted of any scarce item, such as certain types of shells. For at least the last four thousand years, coins made out of precious metal, most often gold, silver, or copper, have been made to serve as money. The value of any item could be described in relation to a standard silver or gold coin. This relation is known as the "price" (e.g., ten silver coins equal one cow).

Coins were easier to carry and more standardized than cows or wheat, and hence were a better medium of exchange and settlement, and unit of account. Coins could be standardized as to metallic content, size, and weight, and coins made

---

creditors may not agree universally which assets discharge obligations. Food stamps, Canadian dollars, cigarettes, and $100 bills are all assets which are accepted as payment at some times and locations but not at other times and locations. In other cases, an asset may be accepted for payment but not at face value.

Media of settlement refer to the assets or commodities which are delivered to extinguish the legal claims that the payee has upon the payor. Under a traditional gold standard, for instance, gold is a medium of settlement, although both gold coins and dollars are media of exchange. Dollars can be used to retire debts but dollars remain a claim to some further asset, namely, gold. A medium of settlement is defined by contracts and legal and business conventions.

Marketability is a concept closely related to media of exchange and settlement and refers to the ease of selling an asset or commodity; we treat the terms liquidity and saleability as synonymous with marketability. Individuals incur different types of costs when trying to sell exchange media. Selling costs may involve bid-ask spreads, the time required to find buyers, and the price buyers will pay for exchange media. Assets do not possess intrinsic degrees of marketability. Instead, the marketability of assets depends upon the qualities of goods and assets, information about asset value, transactions technologies for pricing these assets, and the regulatory regime.

Finally, we distinguish between a unit of account and a medium of account. A *medium of account* is a standard in which prices or debts are quoted. Media of account are usually commodities or assets, although we consider also "ghost" or "abstract" media of account. Currently, the medium of account in the United States is the dollar; during the gold standard era the medium of account in

out of rare metals, such as gold, proved to be a good store of value.

Gold and silver coins were a good but not perfect money. They could be clipped or adulterated. They could be subject to deflation or inflation if the costs of new production of the metal varied significantly from the costs of previous production. A big gold find could drive down the price of gold in relation to other goods, resulting in inflation, or a dearth of new finds could result in deflation as the price of gold rose in comparison to other goods. Both inflation and deflation destabilize the existing economic order, and instability tends to reduce real incomes for some period of time (from what they would otherwise be). Coins also have the disadvantage of being cumbersome for large purchases, and they are easily stolen.

The invention of paper currency overcame some of the disadvantages of coins.[9] Paper was lighter, easier to transport, could be made in any denomination and was far less costly to produce than coins. In most countries, early paper currency was totally backed by gold or silver coins or bullion, so it was no more subject to inflation or deflation than gold or silver coins. But both private banks that issued money and government officials soon learned that they could print more of the

---

the United States was gold. The medium of account name, however, may not be expressed directly on the price tag. Under the gold standard, for instance, merchants at times were willing to accept a certain quantity of dollars (defined in terms of gold), rather than a certain number of gold ounces, as would be required in a strict gold clause contract.

A *unit of account* refers to a specific quantity of a medium of account, that is, the units in which prices are posted. The unit of account under the American gold standard was the dollar, which referred not just to gold in general but to a particular quantity of gold, specifically 1.5046 grams of a specified purity. Unit of account choice involves issues of denominations; for instance, should a merchant price his product at "one dollar" or "four quarters"? Medium of account choice occurs when a merchant decides whether to price at "one dollar" defined in terms of gold versus "one dollar" defined in terms of silver.

[9]In 1295, Marco Polo brought word of China's paper currency—the world's first— back to Europe. The first government outside China to issue paper currency, however, was that of the Massachusetts colony, which created it in 1690 to pay for a military expedition ordered by London. The first modern preprinted checks, which depositors could use to pay anyone, appeared in England in 1781." (From "Money Fact," Discover, October 1998, 84).

currency than they had gold or silver to back it. These systems were called fractional reserve systems when there was still some gold or silver backing, or fiat systems when there was no metal or other real backing. (Fractional reserve also applies to banks, when the central bank sets the portion—less than 100%—of reserves a bank must hold against deposits.) As long as government officials could convince the public that they were not printing any more currency than they had the ability to collect in additional tax revenue, inflation would not occur. Remember, government-issued money is a liability of the government to the person holding the money.

However, the problem is that politicians and government officials tend to obtain power by spending someone else's money on their favorite constituents. At the same time, citizens do not like paying the taxes necessary to support the politicians' spending desires. Politicians, looking for the quick fix, figured out that if they merely printed more money they could tax less and spend more—ah, nirvana! But printing more money does present a problem if the government cannot sell enough bonds (government debt) at reasonable rates of interest to offset the increase in money growth.[10] Then one has the situation in which there is too much money chasing too few goods, also known as inflation. Politicians, being politicians, may try to blame the inflation that they have caused on "greedy business people" raising prices. The fact is that *significant* inflation has always been and always will be a monetary phenomenon. If the government produces the money, it and it alone causes inflation—not some sort of collective greed.

Unfortunately for the politician, most people do not like inflation because of the simple fact that their savings lose value

---

[10]Printing money is not inflationary (in the first order) if the government borrows from the market by selling bonds to cover the printed money, which extinguishes an equal quantity of money. Unfortunately, in the real world more monetary growth is often accompanied by more government spending.

and money cannot buy as much as it did previously and thus, uncertainty in their lives grows. After some period of high inflation, people tend to disbelieve political leaders who tell them that someone else is responsible for the drop in their money's value. This realization on the part of the people tends to limit the political lifetimes of political leaders. Despite the fact that paper money has been used for three centuries, and that the world has experienced hundreds of inflationary episodes, these lessons are still being learned.

The Future of Money

The good news is that we are now about to enter a glorious age when people will not have to endure episodes of sustained inflation. People can have a choice of monies, both government-issued and privately-issued monies, which will enable them to escape from unstable money. If a government central bank, such as the US Federal Reserve Bank, engages in an inflationary monetary policy, users of its money will switch to a different currency or will hold other assets. People will still be forced to use government money for the payment of taxes and for the receipt of payments from government. But, for private transactions, people will increasingly move away from government money.[11] Governments that produce money with a stable value (no or little inflation), will find that their money may be used as a unit of account and medium of settlement, even though it may not be used as a store of value or a medium of exchange.

There are a series of technological and regulatory changes underway that will eventually make privately-issued digital (electronic) money the norm. These changes will alleviate the

---

[11]Those who use money-like instruments other than the legal tender of their own government may be subject to capital gains liabilities, which in turn may slow the movement away from government money.

many problems experienced with conventional central bank-issued money, and particularly with paper currency and coins, which were noted above.

Credit cards have become popular in the developed, high-income countries over the last several decades. Many people think of their credit card as money, because it fills many of the same functions. More recently, debit cards that deduct funds from one's checking account have become popular. Credit and debit cards reduce the need for a person to carry currency or to write checks. In fact, it has become almost impossible to travel internationally without them, because airlines, hotels, and car rental agencies often insist that you use them for payment and/or identification. Credit and debit cards provide a complete tracking of all the expenditures made on them, both for the user and others, such as banks and government agencies.

The card issuers also require the merchants who accept them to have an on-line verification system to make sure the user has the credit line or sufficient funds in the bank account to cover the intended purchase. This verification is done over a telephone line using a specialized electronic device called a "point-of-sale terminal" (POS). For example, if you wish to pay a hotel bill in London (or anywhere else in the world) using a Visa card, the hotel clerk takes your card and puts it in a POS, which then sends the account name and number, and the transaction information, over the phone lines, satellite or wireless (depending upon the locally available communication infrastructure and its perceived reliability according to Visa's technical requirements). The information is then sent to one of the four Visa centers in California (USA), Virginia (USA), Basingstoke (UK), or Yokohama (Japan). A redundancy system is available for protection in case one system is down. The Visa centers verify the card and the amount of credit or debit, and send a confirmation or denial back over the satellite to the hotel in London. All of this is accomplished in under ten seconds, while the information processing time inside the Visa global system is only two seconds (the ten-second estimate is based on dial-up time and the time to enter the Visa global system, over which Visa has no control). The cost of this is only about fifteen cents per transaction, but it does require reliable communications service.

Credit and debit cards have a magnetic stripe on the back, which is machine readable, but the magnetic stripe is rather limited in the amount of data it contains. But, because of the necessary telephone hookup and the lack of anonymity, and the cost for very small purchases, credit and debit cards will never become universal payment mechanisms.

There is a technology that can overcome the limitations of credit and debit cards—the "smart card." The smart card is another piece of plastic that resembles a credit or debit card, but it contains a computer microchip. This chip can contain and process a considerable amount of information.[12] Monetary value can be downloaded into the card and stored, and then deducted in increments as purchases are made. The machine that adds and subtracts information into the card chip is known as a smart card reader/writer. These are small and inexpensive and can be easily installed in ATM machines, PC's, and telephones. When you use a smart card as a "cash purse," you will download money from your bank account into the card in the same way you withdraw cash from an ATM machine. Each time you make a purchase from the card, the amount of the purchase is deducted from the value of the card and deposited in the merchant's computer through a reader/writer.

The smart card can be used to make very small purchases,

---

[12] The newest cards have chips which have 64 kilobytes of storage space. This number will likely continue to rise as better cards are developed.

such as buying a newspaper or a soft drink from a vending machine, or larger payments, such as hotel bills or airline tickets. In countries like the US, government authorities and the card-issuing organizations will limit the amount of money (actually, the claim on money in the bank) that can be downloaded into the card. These limits typically range from $100 to $2,500. Some countries will have much higher or even no limits on cards issued in their jurisdictions. The cards can be made secure by such identification devices as pin codes, fingerprints, handprints, or even voice prints. Some smart card systems are anonymous; others provide a payments record. Some systems allow the money in the card to be passed from card to card outside of the banking system, whereas others require each transaction to be cleared through the banking system before the "smart (digital) money" can be used again. Smart card transactions are far less costly—under three cents per transaction—than credit or debit cards, checks, or even cash. They are almost impossible to counterfeit, and to a thief they are far less appealing than cash.

Smart cards also have the advantage that they are far more durable than paper currency, and physically they can last a number of years. Unlike currency and coins, they are not handled by many strangers and hence are cleaner, and they are less bulky to carry. Cards, like coins and currency, are subject to loss and theft. However, if a card with a good security device (e.g., pin code) is stolen, it cannot be used by others, thus reducing the incentive for theft. Indeed, those card systems that require bank clearing after each transaction, as contrasted with anonymous smart card-to-card systems, enable the holder to recoup the remaining balance in the card when it is lost or stolen.

Unlike paper currency and coins, the debit, credit, and smart card systems require that merchants and others who accept them have machines that can read the cards (*i.e.*, point-of-sale terminals). Fortunately, card reader/writers can be made very small and are inexpensive to produce, so they can be easily fitted in an ATM machine, vending machine, telephone or computer, or even carried in one's pocket. A bigger problem has been agreeing on the technological standards so that merchants do not have to have multiple card reader/writers for different cards and systems. Progress is being made in establishing international standards for credit and debit smart cards. These standards (referred to as the EMV standards) are being developed by Europay, Master-Card, and Visa. In July 1998, American Express Company and Visa International set up a joint venture to develop a worldwide, open standard for smart cards. The joint venture company will "develop the technology and standards that would allow a single piece of plastic to perform a variety of applications such as storage of electronic money, credit or debit card, access to mobile-phone or cable-TV networks and settlement of Internet transactions."[13] Eventually, worldwide standards are likely to develop, allowing people to use the same card worldwide.[14]

---

[13]Martin DuBois and Douglas Lavin, "American Express, Visa Form Smart-Card Unit," Wall Street Journal, 20 July 1998, B6.

[14]Visa International, along with First Union Bank, was the first to widely market SmartCard Technology in the US. From October 1995 through the 1996 Summer Olympics in Atlanta, over one million Visa Cash cards were manufactured. Visa Cash Smart Cards are in wide use throughout Atlanta. They are used by Metro Atlanta Rapid Transit, colleges, sports stadiums, United Artists Cinemas, General Cinemas and the United States Army, in lieu of cash transactions. (From the Visa Cash home page).

The Visa Smart Card user may purchase a set dollar amount, or use a reloadable Smart Card known as a SmartCheck Card or Smart 24-hour card. Going to an ATM would reload the user's Smart 24-hour card. Using the SmartCard takes approximately 1-6 seconds, while a cash transaction takes 30-40 seconds.

The Mondex Smart Card has been available since July 1995 as a pilot project. The Mondex card supports up to 5 currencies, is lockable, and will transfer over telephone lines. There are no charges for the pilot project. There is a maximum of 500 pounds sterling per transaction.

Hardware items that are available for use with Mondex include: Mondex Card, Mondex retailer terminal, Mondex wallet, a balance reader, Mondex telephone (to transfer money to other Mondex cardholders worldwide), and Mondex ATM. The Mondex wallet is a pocket-size unit which can also store digital money. It is intended to store higher amounts of digital money to be transferred to the card. It also enables individuals to make money transfers between cards. Consumers only need carry the Mondex Card. (From http://www.ict.tuwien.ac.at/eipan/cikersch/mo.html).

Mondex launched a pilot project in New York in October 1997, on Manhattan's upper West Side. It is a joint venture, with MasterCard, Visa, Citibank, and Chase Manhattan Bank participating. Chase Manhattan and Citibank are offering Mondex electronic cash and the Visa Cash stored value product, respectively. Over 600 merchants participate in the

However, electronic payments do not need to be made from a smart card; they can be made directly from a computer. In the same way that money is downloaded from a bank account into a smart card, it can be downloaded directly to the hard drive of a PC. The "money" on the hard drive can then be sent to someone else's PC and hence to his bank account. All of these transactions can be secured by utilizing virtually unbreakable public key encryption.[15] (See Chapter III for a more detailed discussion of encryption).

As a result of the technologies described above, all of which are already operational, it is possible to send "money" from one point to another point on the globe, at almost the speed of light, and anonymously. These funds transfers can be sent in an encrypted format that is, for all practical purposes, unbreakable and totally secure from any criminal or government.

As advanced as smart cards are becoming, they are only an interim step in the digital information age. Though it sounds like science fiction, serious work is underway to develop various types of microchip implants for the human body. Some are being developed for medical reasons, and others for identification and information reasons. Tests have already been conducted with implants in the human body. Most body implants will be so small as not to be readily noticed, and the implant process is eventually likely to be even less traumatic than having one's ear pierced. At some point in the future, a significant portion of the information, insurance, and money-

---

program, accepting electronic cash for payment of a variety of goods. MasterCard and Visa have worked so that both Mondex and VisaCash can be used at the same businesses, in the same way that competing credit cards are accepted. (From the Mondex website at http://www.mondex.com/mondex/cgi-bin/printpage.pl?english+global&pilots_newyork_1.html)

[15]Public key encryption refers to a system where a private person gives a code, "the public key" (which may be published), to those who are interested in sending the code issuer an encrypted message. Public key encryption should not be confused with government "key escrow" account systems. These government "key escrow" systems require that encryption keys be placed into an escrow account for the government to access if they believe that information about a crime has been hidden by encryption.

like items (*i.e.*, cash and credit cards) that most people keep in
their wallets will almost certainly be carried in the form of
"implants." These implants will be sufficiently small, benign,
and non-intrusive (even less so than much of the current fad in
body-piercing jewelry) that many people will prefer them.
There will be no more concern about losing one's wallet or
proving one's identity. Financial transactions will be made by
a voice instruction or the wave of a hand.

We are entering an age when governments will not be able
to trace the money transactions of those who wish anonymity.
Previously, this had only been true for cash transactions. Cash
is bulky and hard to hide and therefore frequently detected.[16]
This new technological reality will force governments to
change their tax systems and the techniques they use to detect
criminal activity. The open question is whether they will
engage in constructive change by reducing taxes on capital and
reducing their attempts at financial intrusion, or resort to
destructive change by criminalizing the activities of a significant
portion of their populations.

Why Government Will Lose its Monopoly on Money Creation

*There is no subtler, no surer means of overturning the exist-
ing basis of society than to debauch the currency.*

–John Maynard Keynes

The government monopoly on money is a recent innovation. In the US, the government monopoly on money was
only established in 1913 with the creation of the Federal

---

[16]According to the Justice Department's calculations, 1 million dollars in $100 bill denomina-
tions weighs 22 lbs. (Figures cited in Douglas Farah's article, "Moving Mountains of Illicit Cash,"
Washington Post, 9 August 1997).

Reserve System. Up to that time private banks could also issue currency, which were private dollar-denominated bank notes. Before the Federal Reserve, the government defined the dollar in terms of the amount of gold and/or silver needed to acquire one dollar. Those large Eastern US banks which were known to have substantial reserves were able to issue their bank notes at par. For example, a dollar note from Chase Bank in New York was considered as good as a dollar note from the US Treasury. Smaller banks, particularly in the American West, whose reliability was in doubt, found that they could only sell their one dollar bank notes at a discount. Those banks that were less well known outside of their home regions, although sound, also tended to sell bank notes at a discount because of the lack of good and widespread information. Another major problem with the plethora of different bills issued was that it was relatively easier to produce counterfeit notes that would not be detected. According to one account, "It is estimated that about one-third of all notes in circulation in the US during that period were counterfeit."[17]

Given the desire for riskless money, governments acquired monopoly rights. Most often it was central banks that issued the money that was made "legal tender." Legal tender laws obligated others to accept the government money for all financial obligations, and required taxes to be paid in the government money. Most people prefer government-issued money, because of the belief that governments do not go broke, and because having one currency simplifies monetary transactions. The preference for government money, however, declines as inflation rises.

Governments like having the monopoly on money issuance because, to the extent that they are able to produce the currency at less cost than the face value of the currency, they

---

[17]Warren Coats and Charles Kelly, "The Simple Analytics of Digital Money: Finance in Cyberspace," (International Monetary Fund. August 1996 Draft paper), 9.

receive a profit known as "seigniorage." In addition, because the money itself is a debt owed by the government to the holder of the currency, and there is no interest accruing on this debt, the government is getting an interest-free loan. Thus, money issuance is very profitable because of the seigniorage and float. In 1996, the US Federal Reserve System made a net profit of 21 billion dollars, mainly from money issuance. This profit was turned over to the US Treasury. (In practice it merely reduced the amount the Treasury had to borrow). This seigniorage directly results from the government having a monopoly on the issuance of money.

Obviously, private companies seek ways to get part of this profit. The American Express Company makes substantial profits from the issuance of travelers checks. When you purchase a travelers check, you are giving the American Express Company an interest-free loan until the time you cash the check. The smart card used as a cash purse provides the same profit opportunity—interest-free float—to the issuer as does the travelers check. As a result, banks and other issuers of smart cards have an enormous incentive to issue large numbers of smart cards and encourage people to hold money balances on them. In essence, smart card issuers are reducing the public's demand for government-issued currency, thus shifting the profits from the government to the private sector.

Competition among private financial institutions and others to obtain profits from money issuance, or from providing money substitutes, is driving down the cost of transactions and eroding the central banks' "market share" and control of the functions of money. As we enter into the digital age, private competitors to central banks will be in an increasingly advantageous situation, despite legal tender laws.

For a couple of decades, companies such as Merrill Lynch have offered "money management accounts" and similar products.

These accounts, as well as many mutual funds today, enable people to write checks against their securities accounts. Over time, most securities accounts deliver far higher rates of return than bank accounts, particularly very low interest checking accounts. Thus it makes sense for people to shift from non-interest-bearing or low-interest-bearing accounts to higher return accounts or assets, if they can do so while still having high liquidity.

If you could avoid holding any (non-interest bearing) currency or coin at all, and still have the same, or greater, ease and ability to spend, you would probably choose to do so. Further, if you could keep your assets in a form where they make higher rather than lower rates of return, commensurate with whatever level of risk you are willing to accept, you probably would choose to do so. Finally, if you could take your liquid assets, such as your stock portfolio, and your illiquid assets, such as your home, and turn part of their value into money only at the moment you wish to purchase some other good or service, you would also probably choose to do that.

In fact, we are rapidly reaching the point where you will be able to do all of the above. Many business firms and some individuals are already partially turning their assets into money only at the moment they need to make an expenditure. They do this by obtaining a line of credit from the bank, using their assets as collateral. When they need to purchase something, they write a check or have an electronic transfer made against the line of credit. In this case, the bank credit performs many of the functions of money. It makes economic sense for the business to operate in this way when the rate of return it receives on its assets is greater than the cost of the line of credit from the bank.

Debit cards often are issued against interest-bearing accounts. Smart cards, which combine the capabilities of a prepaid and debit card, can also be interest bearing. (This is only true with some smart systems; it is not necessarily applicable to those systems that allow anonymous card-to-card transfers.) Almost all electronic money will be interest bearing. Therefore, central bank money almost certainly will decline in importance because of its lack of competitiveness.

What is most likely to develop is that the primary issuers of electronic money in the future will be mutual funds. Mutual funds, by having diverse and liquid assets, can offer less risk than traditional banks. With a mutual fund, holders can cash in all or part of their ownership of the fund at any time, but not at a fixed price. Thus the mutual fund account is as liquid as a demand account deposit at a bank. (There are some exceptions, such as a "hedge fund"—in which the participants cannot withdraw their capital or capital obligation before a specified time or only with the permission of the management of the fund.) In some countries, mutual fund shareholders already can write checks and request electronic transfers to third parties against their share balance.

Mutual funds also have the advantage that they are not subject to bank runs resulting from a loss of confidence in the bank. A bank can find itself in a position where its obligations to depositors are greater than the assets of the bank. Given that bank deposits have a par value, the first people in the withdrawal queue receive 100% of their deposits, and the ones left in the queue after the bank's funds run out get nothing if there is no deposit insurance, or get their funds only after a long wait if deposit insurance exists.

Under the mutual fund, increases and decreases in share values in the underlying securities portfolio of the fund are distributed (actually, "marked to market[18]") on an equal pro-rata basis to all the holders of the fund. The value of the fund may decline, and so each fund holder shares the same percentage decline, as contrasted with the bank deposit "all or nothing" par value system. What this means is that a holder of a mutual fund share has more risk than a holder of an insured bank account, but this risk is offset by the greater returns the mutual fund holder normally receives. So-called money market mutual funds (which hold highly rated government and corporate debt obligations) are available for those seeking little risk but still higher returns than normal demand accounts.

Another major financial innovation that will accelerate the movement to non-governmental money is securitization. This is the process by which previously illiquid assets are made liquid. An example of securitization would be a financial company that pools a group of loans and then sells claims on these loans to borrowers. In the United States, organizations like "Fannie Mae" pool home mortgages and sell them to financial institutions, mutual funds, and wealthy individuals. An increasingly wide variety of assets are now securitized. For instance, the expected stream of royalties from singer David Bowie's recordings have been securitized. In theory, virtually any marketable asset could be securitized.

As previously mentioned, given that owners of mutual fund shares are easily able to draw down their claims on the real assets in the mutual fund, *and with electronic transfer the claim can be settled on a real time basis,*[19] there is none of the risk to either party in the transaction that could result from a delayed settlement. Substantial progress already has been made in establishing real time settlements. For instance, the Swiss instituted the Swiss Interbank Clearing system back in 1987, which was in part the model for the European Union

---

[18]"Marked to market" is simply the term for valuing a portfolio on the basis of current market prices.

[19]A "real time" settlement basis just means that the settlement is complete at the time of transaction, comparable to a cash payment.

real time gross settlement system (RTGS) that recently was established. As Browne and Cronin explained:

> ... the development of securitized banking and instantaneous settlement by electronic transfer seem capable of realising what in the monetary economics literature is known as a "pure accounting system of exchange". Under such a payments system, transactions are effected by means of signals to an accounting network resulting in appropriate credits and debits to wealth accounts of buyers and sellers. These signals will be as close to instantaneous as makes no material difference, *i.e.*, all retail payments are transacted in real time, in which case there will, of course, be no need for a whole interbank clearing system. With an accounting exchange system, the tangible money of monetary exchange systems will be missing yet the gross inefficiencies of primitive barter will be obviated. ... The creditworthiness of the purchaser can be instantaneously verified by the vendor through the immediate, but restricted, electronic access to the purchaser's wealth account. Such a facility would nullify one of the hitherto clear advantages of currency as a transactions medium, namely, that authentication and verification of the creditworthiness of a purchaser using currency is not necessary.[20]

In sum, the new electronic payment technologies allow holders of assets to earn interest or other returns on these assets up to the moment when they transfer the ownership of a portion of the assets to pay for a good or service.

---

[20]Frank Browne and David Cronin, "How Technology is Likely to Mould the Future Shape of Banking," The Irish Banking Review, August 1994, 17.

As more "money" becomes interest-bearing electronic money, there is less inflation risk, because there is no incentive for private banks or other financial institutions to over-issue interest-bearing currency since it increases their own liabilities. (This is because the issuance of interest-bearing "money" makes the issuer not only liable for the principal, but also for the interest. Governments producing non-interest-bearing money, such as currency, do not have this liability for the interest, and therefore in the first order they seem to be getting something for nothing. Thus, there is an incentive for the government to produce more non-interest bearing currency than they would otherwise). The unit of account (e.g., the US dollar) will probably continue to be set by the central bank, even though the use of government money as a transaction medium will decline. But the government will only be able to hold on to its function of establishing a unit of account if it operates in a non-inflationary or deflationary manner. Governments increasingly are being disciplined by the market because, in the age of instant global communications and financial institutions, any increase in inflation immediately causes a capital and currency flight. The Asian financial crisis of 1997 is a good example of how rapidly capital can move from an economy once investors lose faith in a government. Capital flight has a strong negative effect on the real economy, which then causes a political backlash.

Governments increasingly have to compete with other governments and private providers of monetary numeraires (e.g., the US dollar, Japanese Yen, British Pound, Swiss Franc). Eventually, some governments probably will define their currency's value explicitly in the form of a tradable basket of goods and services. Commodities that are traded on organized commodity futures exchanges, having a one world price, are prime candidates. For example, the dollar might be defined as x amount of gold, plus y amount of crude oil, plus z amount of corn. This would be nothing more than a modern version of the old gold standard, but the basket of goods and services will more clearly reflect what the world both produces and consumes, and whose characteristics are easily measured—metals, agricultural products, energy products, and even such things as insurance rates. The Federal Reserve Board under Chairman Alan Greenspan is known to have implicitly followed sensitive commodity prices, such as gold and oil, in the determination of the US monetary policy. When the Fed deviated from this policy in 1998, by letting the price of the "basket" of sensitive commodity prices fall, including gold in dollar terms, it was forced to play "catch up."[21] These implicit rules most likely will become more explicit over time.

If governments fail to develop explicit definitions of the value of their currencies, the private sector will. Commodity and securities indexes that are presently traded are a step in the direction of producing definitions that could serve the unit of account function of money.

In the economy of the future, most wealth will become both divisible and liquid, and instantaneously transferable, and hence will be useable as transactions media. Since there will be no need to withdraw wealth-producing assets to provide purchasing power, as in a monetary economy, and assuming the unit of account is defined by a specific additive quantity of goods and services, there will be no pressures to produce inflation or deflation. All of the requirements to facilitate trade will still be met, and improved upon.

[21]The Fed attempted to increase the supply of dollars through interest-rate reductions in order to stop the commodity price deflation. Given that commodity prices are flexible and wages are far less so, when commodity prices drop, the ratio between wages and prices increases, thus causing an apparent rise in wages. This apparent rapid increase in the relative price of labor causes businesses to slow hiring or engage in layoffs, which in turn slows or even reverses economic growth. Thus, "deflation" can be as harmful to economic growth as "inflation" because both cause unanticipated changes in relative prices and distort the price signals the economy needs to operate efficiently. In the digital world, private producers of monetary numeraires will gain acceptance for their products if the producers of government monies fail to maintain constant measures of purchasing power—that is, if they allow their money to either "inflate" or "deflate."

The Need for Monetary Freedom

When one studies the history of money one cannot help wondering why people should have put up for so long with governments exercising an exclusive power over 2,000 years that was regularly used to exploit and defraud them.

—F. A. Hayek[22]

In this new digital world, transaction costs will be sharply reduced, leading to higher income levels for the world's people. Now that the technological problems have been solved, the speed at which people acquire the benefits of the non-monetary economy will depend largely on how fast governments get out of the way. The new technologies will not be widely accepted unless people believe they are secure in their transactions, and know that they have the financial privacy and anonymity that cash now provides. This means that governments will need to abolish their controls on encryption (which cannot be enforced anyway), and get away from the notion that they have a right to monitor people's spending and investing behavior.

In a world largely without "money," the notion of money laundering as a crime becomes absurd. Tax evasion and such other criminal activities as drug dealing are the real crimes (if society chooses to outlaw them), not the use of money from these activities. Trying to monitor these crimes by monitoring the use of money is difficult, and harmful for the efficiency of money. New technology increases the difficulty of monitoring, so other less destructive and more direct means of fighting crime should be developed. The fact is, whether well-intentioned or ill-intentioned, government policy makers and

---

[22]F. A. Hayek, <u>Denationalisation of Money—The Argument Refined</u>, 3d. ed., The Institute for Economic Affairs (Lancing, Sussex: Goron Pro-Print Co. Ltd., 1990), 33.

bureaucrats who defend the encryption controls and money laundering statutes are denying the peoples of the world better living standards and a higher level of freedom.

Chapter III

THE CASE FOR FINANCIAL PRIVACY

*Experience should teach us to be most on our guard to
protect liberty when the government's purposes are
beneficent ... the greatest dangers to liberty lurk
in insidious encroachment by men of zeal,
well-meaning but without understanding.*

— Justice Louis D. Brandeis

Financial privacy is about the ability, and what many consider the right, to keep confidential the facts concerning one's income, expenditures, investments and wealth. Without financial privacy, many other fundamental freedoms, such as freedom of religion and speech, are endangered. Invasions of financial privacy are common characteristics of virtually all abusive governments.

Those who would limit or eliminate financial freedom often argue that, if you have nothing to hide and are only engaged in lawful activities, you should not object to full disclosure of your financial activities. Such an argument fails to understand the basic nature of man for without privacy there is no personal life, and the kind of civil society most people seek is probably not possible. Princess Diana had almost everything but privacy, and that lack of privacy clearly caused her misery. Chekhov expressed it more cynically in "Lady with the Dog," writing: "The personal life of every individual is based on secrecy, and perhaps it is partly for that reason that civilized man is so nervously anxious that personal privacy should be respected."

Even those who have only a modest acquaintance with world history should observe that the most civilized and tolerant societies have had a high regard for privacy of all sorts. The most brutish and intolerant societies have had no respect for privacy. Thoughtful people realize that this is no coincidence. Totalitarian regimes always target the privacy of their subjects.

Those who advocate financial disclosure also seem to have no understanding that people have the right, and all too often the need, to protect themselves from corrupt or abusive elements within governments, assorted criminals and potential wrongdoers, or just downright nasty or insensitive people. The right of self-defense is as basic a human right as there is. Those who would strip away financial privacy are also cutting away at the right of self-defense.

Financial privacy cannot be isolated and stripped from other forms of human privacy. In the modern world, man's means of providing food, shelter, and self-esteem are mostly translated into financial concepts—money, earnings, spending, investing, and wealth. The details of a person's financial life are telling indicators of his religious practices, sexual activities, and political preferences. Once all this is public knowledge, not much privacy is left. As Disraeli said, knowledge is power. If you know everything about a person's finances, including the nature and sources of his income, you have power over that person.

The Historical Case for Privacy

They that can give up essential liberty to obtain a little temporary safety deserve neither safety nor liberty.

—Benjamin Franklin

Those who argue for free financial disclosure to our government, on the notion that the people who serve in the US government are only interested in protecting us from evil, are both naïve and dangerous. That notion is totally contrary to the facts.

We are told that the information given to the government will remain confidential. The law requires that IRS and FBI files shall not be disclosed. Yet we know that sensitive files have been disclosed by a number of Administrations over the past fifty years, often for political reasons. Under the Clinton Administration, FBI files were given to unauthorized people for political purposes, and there have been extensive and well-reported abuses at the IRS. Only after an embarrassing Congressional investigation did the IRS apologize. The Deputy Treasury Secretary, Roger Altman, and the General Counsel of the Treasury, Jean Hanson, both had to resign in disgrace because they abused privacy. Do you really want people like this knowing the intimate details of your financial life? Nearly every Administration has been plagued by some officials who violated the public trust. Given that not everyone who serves in government is a saint, it is only realistic to expect that despite laws and regulations, some government officials at some time will violate citizens' legal privacy if they have access to sensitive information.

Some might recall that when Judge Robert Bork went before the US Senate in his confirmation hearings, a Senate staffer had managed to obtain records of his video-tape rentals. If we get to the point where we know the intimate financial details of everyone who is up for elective office or high appointive office, will anyone pass muster, other than the most boring, bland, and unimaginative? Civilization has not progressed because of the activities of the bland and unimaginative.

The American Constitution is based on the idea of limited government. Until the passage of the Sixteenth Amendment in 1913, which gave us the income tax, there was no constitutional authority for any invasion of financial privacy. Alexis de Tocqueville, in his classic work of 1848, <u>Democracy in America</u>, observed: "The lot of the Americans is singular: they have derived from the aristocracy of England the notion of private rights and the taste for local freedom; and they have been able to retain both because they have no aristocracy to combat."[23]

Some legal scholars argue that the existing requirements, as well as new demands for financial disclosure, conflict with the Fourth Amendment to the Constitution, which states:

> The right of the people to be secure in their persons, houses, paper, and effects, against unreasonable searches and seizures, shall not be violated, and no Warrants shall issue, but beyond probable cause, supported by Oath or affirmation, and particularly describing the place

---

[23]Alexis de Tocqueville, <u>Democracy in America</u> Vol. 2. (Vintage Press, 1945), 316.

to be searched, and the persons or things to be seized.

Quite obviously, the IRS could not exist in its present form if the Fourth Amendment were still literally interpreted as the law of the land, rather than the Sixteenth.

Why Financial Privacy Is Moral

The right to possess private property is derived from nature, not from man; and the state has by no means the right to abolish it.

—Pope Leo XIII

The Swiss, and others who have bank privacy laws, have been under attack for years by officials and critics in countries that do not have bank privacy laws. Nations that do not have bank privacy (such as the US) are at a competitive disadvantage to those countries that do offer bank privacy, and that attract deposits from around the world. Officials from countries that do not offer bank privacy often cloak self-interested attacks on their competitors in high-sounding moral rhetoric. For instance, they suggest that Swiss bank privacy only exists to protect drug dealers and international criminals. In fact, Swiss banking laws do not protect money from criminal sources. These laws were tightened in the 1980s and 1990s to meet the strictest international standards. Criminals who wish to disguise the origins of their wealth sometimes shelter behind the attorney-client privilege and use their lawyers to evade these laws, but this problem is being addressed by lawmakers in Switzerland and neighboring countries. Critics of bank privacy cannot imagine, it seems, that anyone but a criminal would be interested in keeping his affairs to himself.

Policy makers in the US have long argued against bank privacy on the basis that the IRS needed access to individuals' and businesses' banking records. Law enforcement authorities also have argued that they need access to bank records to find and document criminal wrongdoing. These arguments have a certain initial appeal—until you look closely at Switzerland. Is this government unable to collect taxes?[24] Is Switzerland overrun with criminals? No, it is a peaceful, prosperous country.

The Swiss have been attacked because some of their banks did not make adequate efforts to find the heirs of victims of the Holocaust and return the assets that these victims deposited in Swiss banks. In part because of the Cold War, these bankers claimed that they had found it virtually impossible to trace the heirs of dormant accounts whose original owners had resided in Poland, Czechoslovakia, Romania, and other then-Eastern-Bloc countries. Bankers were also too rigid in demanding the same proofs of ownership from Holocaust survivors as one would expect from ordinary claimants of dormant accounts. Thankfully, world opinion has awakened the conscience of the banking community, which is finally making vigorous efforts to locate the rightful heirs of these accounts.

Unfortunately, there also has been much hypocrisy in this attack on the Swiss. Many of these attacks have come from countries that did far less than the Swiss to protect both the assets and the lives of the Jewish refugees, particularly in relation to the size of their populations. Ironically, the Swiss bank privacy laws were established explicitly to protect individuals persecuted by their governments. The Swiss have a long tradition of sheltering refugees and their assets, dating back to the seventeenth century, when Geneva and Basel welcomed

---

[24]Switzerland's total tax revenue as a percent of GDP is one of the lowest of the OECD, while the proportion of direct taxes is much higher in Switzerland than in most other countries.

Protestants fleeing persecution in France. During the French revolution, aristocrats (along with their wealth) escaping the Jacobins found refuge in Switzerland. So it was not surprising that Jews and other victims of Nazi persecution looked to Switzerland as a safe place to protect their assets from confiscation.[25]

The much-maligned Swiss bank privacy laws were enacted in 1934 to protect Germans and Jews who were trying to place their funds beyond Hitler's grasp. Many German Jews had placed assets in Switzerland.[26] It was widely assumed that Switzerland would eventually fall to Germany's advance through Europe, and thus, many people were using Swiss accounts as a temporary measure and transit point to send their assets to more remote and presumably safer regions such as the United States, Great Britain, and Brazil. As Hitler was in the process of suppressing German civil liberties, he promulgated a law ordering all citizens to declare their foreign holdings, under penalty of death. Hitler sent agents of the Gestapo to Switzerland in an attempt to identify the German accounts.

---

[25]It has recently been revealed that some of the German Jewish refugees who fled to Switzerland were put into labor camps during the war. Some of these refugees have reported cases of abuse, others have said that they were well-treated, and worked no harder than the Swiss working population. Approximately 15% of all the refugees in Switzerland were put in labor camps.

[26]The extent of the concern for the safety and property of those who were fleeing from Nazi persecution is well captured in the following personal reminiscence of a Swiss citizen Jörg Boller, who, as a child, watched the events of the Forties unfold. As he recalls:

In mid-May 1940—before the German Wehrmacht had broken through the Maginot line in Sedan—the rumor kettle was boiling especially in the border regions of Bodensee and Rhein. Intelligence officers in the vicinity of the legendary captain Paul Meyer, alias Wolf Schwertenbach (pseudonym as crime writer), at Castle Wolfsberg in Ermatingen claimed to know of German troop concentrations in Schwarzwald which were ready at any moment to march into Switzerland.

In this hour of extreme uncertainty SKA branch director Witzig called his colleagues and friends and asked them to empty the safe deposit boxes of any objects owned by people who had fled. ... The contents of the boxes would be very insecure in case of a German invasion, which was expected any minute, especially because in many cases valuable Judaica and expensive jewelry by German jewelers were concerned, which was considered by the Germans enemy-of-the-state property and would be seized without any doubt. Those owning the safe deposit boxes were subject to strict sanctions and punishment, as had happened recently in Holland in similar cases.

> Most Germans who had exported capital felt
> they had no choice but to put their trust in the
> Swiss not to reveal information on their personal
> finances, and a great many Germans did not
> report their accounts across the border. ... [The
> Gestapo's] methods and techniques are still de-
> scribed by the Swiss as "diabolical and clever."
> They included not only bribes but efforts to
> deposit funds under suspected account names at
> various Swiss banks. If the funds were accepted
> by a bank, this was considered proof that the
> person named held an account at the bank.[27]

Nevertheless, Swiss banking laws protected the assets, and in some cases the lives, of many innocent people. Power-hungry governments have always seen financial privacy as an obstacle to their attempts to control the lives of individuals. Unlike totalitarians, Americans believe in the sanctity and dignity of the person. As history shows, these qualities can only be protected if the financial privacy of the citizen is guaranteed. Thus financial privacy is profoundly compatible with Western values.

My father and his friends emptied the safe deposit boxes they had rented [for friends who had escaped from Germany]. In my memories I can see that glorious day in May 1940, which left me at 10 years old with an indelible impression. In the evening hours my parents dug a deep pit under a plant tray in the vegetable garden, wrapped jewelry and other valuable objects of their painter friend Heinsheimer in prepared oil cloth, and at the end of their hard work put flower pots and lettuce plants on the grave. My parents had, for my protection, not confided in me, but I could witness this rare event from my wooden hut, and I made it my secret and confessed to my parents only much later, after the return of their friend after the war.

The joy was all the bigger as my father opened the hiding place in front of the eyes of his friend who returned to Switzerland in mid-1945, and could take all valuables and jewelry unharmed and intact from the oil cloth. As thanks, the painter friend left us some paintings, which still occupy an honorary place in my home. All those who had built on the help of their Swiss friends and trusted them with their wealth in the hour of greatest need had similar experiences upon their return. [From Jörg Boller's article, "Aus dem Banksafe in den Garten," [From the Bank Safe to the Garden], Bilanz. Feb. 1997: 80-83.]

[27]Robert Kinsman, Your Swiss Bank Book (Homewood, IL: Dow Jones-Irwin, Inc., 1975), 222.

The Technological Necessity of Financial Privacy

Even apart from the moral case for financial privacy is the technologically-driven certainty of financial privacy. The question is not whether we will have financial privacy—we will. The appropriate question is whether financial privacy will be legal, when, and at what price. The technological genie is out of the bottle. As explained in Chapter I, money as we know it is going to disappear. At some point, all money, and the information money conveys, will be electronic in digital form. Digital money and digital money substitutes will work only if the digital information is encrypted so that it cannot be stolen or misused. Encryption technology has progressed to the point where it is easy for the average person to use encryption for routine transactions. Moreover, encryption programs can be made sufficiently robust that for all practical purposes the encryption is unbreakable, even by governments.

Encryption is the process of taking readable text, and transforming it into text which can only be read by someone who has a key to recreate the original. In its simplest form, this could be an exchange of letters. For instance, if one wanted to write "hello" but have it in code, one could shift each letter three places down the alphabet, and write "khoor." In this example, "hello" is called the "plain text" and "khoor" is the "ciphertext." It is not immediately obvious that the second word stands for hello, but, given the initial rule that each letter has been shifted three places down in the alphabet to arrive at the letter in the ciphertext, a person could work backwards and discover that "khoor" was the encoded text for "hello." Of course, even without being told the rule, with enough samples, a person could deduce it by matching the pattern of encoded text to the most common patterns in the English language, and come up with the original rule. Once someone has done that, any other encoded texts would be easily cracked, and the meaning ascertained. Strong encryption employs rules that are not so easily deduced. In fact, good encryption systems do not rely on the secrecy of the encryption rules at all, but rather on the complexity of the mathematics and random number generators which create the encoding and decoding keys.

Encryption programs generally follow a relatively simple process to code and decode messages. First, an encryption program takes the message (letter, report, etc.), and compresses it, as any simple encoder or compression program does. Then, this compressed file is encrypted, using any of a number of available algorithms. Basically, these are controlled by the use of a key system. There are two options. Either a document can be encrypted making use of a private key, which will also "unlock" or decode the document, or a public key can be used. A public key system employs two keys, one that is readily available to anyone, the "public key," which encrypts the data, and a "private key," which is known only to the person receiving the information. The public-private key system allows correspondents to trade the public key openly, without endangering the security of the document because, even with the public key, a document cannot be decoded. The problem with this system is that it is inherently slow to encrypt and decrypt, particularly if large keys are utilized (because more calculations are needed than in most private key systems). The private key system obviously has the difficulty of transferring the private key to the other correspondent. If there were a secure way to transfer the key, then the information could also be passed in that way.

PGP ("Pretty Good Privacy," a software encryption program) makes use of both key systems. Each time a document is to be sent, the program creates a new private key, referred to as a "session key." This key is used to encode the entire document. The sender's computer then sends this session key to the receiver, first encrypting the session key using the receiver's public key. The receiver's computer receives the encoded session key and decodes it using the receiver's own private key (which requires a passphrase to open). The rest of the document is then decoded using the session key.

In reality, neither the sender nor the receiver knows the session key. A new session key is created each time a document is encrypted, so there is no pattern to look for. Also, this process takes advantage of the speed of private key communications, with the freedom of public key distribution.

On February 27, 1998, the New York Times reported, "Encryption policy has become a flash point because it is both essential for the growth of Internet commerce and vital for the protection of privacy.[28] The US and other governments are trying to limit the strength of encryption that is easily available to that which they can decrypt. Strength is in part determined by the size in bits[29] and generally, the larger the number of bits, the more unbreakable the code. There also are proposals in the US Congress which would allow strong encryption to be available, provided that a special "key" be deposited into an escrow account where it could be accessed by law-enforcement officials to aid in criminal investigations. The problem for

---

[28]John Markoff, "Clinton Continues to Stumble over the 'E' Word (Encryption)," New York Times, 27 February 1998.

[29]A bit is the basic element of information to a computer. It is a single digit, either a 1 or a 0. All complexities and calculations are boiled down to strings of bits, which, in their placement, represent meaningful data and operations.

Numbers are represented in binary form (base 2). The standard system that you use every day is in base 10, and there are ten symbols used to represent the numbers—0, 1, 2, 3, 4, 5, 6, 7, 8, and 9. In base 2, there are only two symbols used, the 0 and the 1. As in base 10, the placement of the symbols (numerals) signifies the number. That is, in base 10, we speak of the ones column, the tens column, the hundreds column, the thousands column, and so on. These are each powers of $10-10^0 = 1$, $10^1 = 10$, $10^2 = 100$, $10^3 = 1000$, and so on. In base 2, we similarly have the ones column, the twos column, the fours column, the eights column, etc. This is exactly parallel to the base 10 example. Here, we have the powers of $2-2^0 = 1$, $2^1 = 2$, $2^2 = 4$, $2^3 = 8$, etc. The following is an example of the first 10 numbers written in base 10 and base 2:

in base 10	0	1	2	3	4	5	6	7	8	9
in base 2	0	1	10	11	100	101	110	111	1000	1001

As you can see, then, a 1 digit number can be represented by up to 4 bits in base 2.

One final note about bits—computer people frequently use the term "bytes." One byte, which comes from the phrase "by eight," is equal to 8 bits.

governments is that the encryption algorithms[30] are now well known, and anyone who is intent upon encrypting a communication that cannot be broken (without the use of an unreasonable amount of computing power) can do so. Thus, the desire of the government to place controls on encryption to aid in law enforcement is fruitless. The New York Times article also noted industry opposition to government controls:

> Silicon Valley executives argue that the law-enforcement demand for the continued ability to wiretap in the information age is wishful thinking at best. The easy availability of powerful encryption software has made it possible for any two people, anywhere in the world to hold a secret conversation beyond the prying of even the most powerful code-breaking computer, they say.[31]

And, as will be explained later in this section, the ability to encrypt a message will always stay ahead of the government's ability to break the encryption code. Thus, the effect of these various proposals to restrict access to encryption is to harm the law-abiding, while merely inconveniencing the criminal. As noted in an article published by the Economist:

> Confidence in encryption is essential for both Internet commerce and the protection of individual privacy. If businesses believe that confidential documents sent over the Internet can be

---

[30]Algorithms are sets of rules used for calculation or problem-solving. In this case, the algorithms are sets of rules followed to create encryption keys, and to encrypt and decrypt texts. It is vital to the encryption industry that encryption algorithms be widely published, and this is because of the necessity of peer review. Any encryption program that states that its algorithm is a secret is likely to be less secure, because fewer individuals have had a chance to find defects, or prove ways to crack the codes. (Remember, the algorithm is just the set of rules, not the keys themselves, so giving away the algorithm is not equivalent to turning over the decryption key.)

[31]John Markoff, "Clinton Continues to Stumble over the 'E' Word (Encryption)," New York Times, 27 February 1998.

hacked into, they won't send them. If credit-card transactions can be easily intercepted, goods will not be purchased. If e-mails that individuals wish to keep private can be electronically steamed open, they will stay unwritten. Powerful encryption is, in fact, an essential protection for the law-abiding. Who would be confident that keys would not get into the wrong hands, that trusted third parties could be trusted or that law-enforcement agencies would not abuse their new powers as they have done old ones, such as phone-tapping?[32]

Government attempts to limit the use of encryption will only further cripple the growth of Internet commerce. Such controls cannot be truly effective in their stated purpose to aid in law enforcement, because of the ubiquitous knowledge of how to create encryption programs.

The US courts have ruled that there can be no restriction on the strength of encryption that may be used by private parties for communication within the US. This is the proper interpretation of the First Amendment's protection of free speech. As discussed earlier, in the digital age, the functions of money will be accomplished by the instantaneous exchange of information that conveys ownership of assets. If the government cannot legally or technologically know the contents of encrypted information sent by electronic means, it cannot know whether a message is a poem exchanged by two lovers or a transfer of $100 million in assets.

Furthermore, encrypted electronic messages sent over the Internet, or by other means, do not recognize national boundaries. For the government to even make a credible attempt to

---

[32]"Privacy on the Internet," Economist, March 7-13, 1998, 19.

monitor financial transactions, given the new technologies, would require such a level of intrusion into the private affairs of people that it would be unacceptable to all but dedicated totalitarians.   The government can, of course, attempt to monitor all transactions through financial institutions, as they presently do in the US, under the cloak of the Bank Secrecy Act. But again, as was explained in Chapter II, exchanges of assets in the future will easily take place outside of the banking system and other non-banking financial institutions.

The new physical reality enormously complicates governmental ambitions.   Present law—whether it is international trade law, intellectual property law, or tax law—is based on the idea of atoms.   The physical world is made up of atoms—automobiles, television sets, books, newspapers, paper currency and coin are all made out of atoms. Governments have learned how to tax and regulate atoms, and the exchange of atoms. But in the digital world there are no atoms, there are only "bits."   As Nicholas Negroponte, Director of MIT's Media Lab, has so clearly explained:

> A bit has no color, size or weight, and it can travel at the speed of light. It is the smallest atomic element in the DNA of information. It is a state of being: on or off, true or false, up or down, in or out, black or white. For practical purposes we consider a bit to be 1 or 0. The meaning of the 1 or 0 is a separate matter. ... Bits have always been the underlying particle of digital computing, but over the past twenty-five years we have greatly expanded our binary vocabulary to include much more than just numbers. We have been able to digitize more and more types of information, like audio and video, rendering them into a similar reduction of 1s and 0s.[33]

Money in smart cards, on computer disks, and sent over the Internet is in the form of digitized information.

When digitized money is encrypted, as virtually all digitized money is and will be, it is unseen. To try to trace it, tax it, and control it is an absurdity. The so-called crime of money laundering will be impossible to enforce in the digital age. Despite the obvious fact that it cannot be enforced any more than the prohibition of alcohol could be enforced, this will not stop those with a police-state mentality from trying. Alcohol is composed of atoms, it has to be contained in a bottle or a can and it is heavy, yet, during Prohibition, only a small percentage of the bootleg product was ever seized or destroyed. The problem of trying to identify "bootleg" money is infinitely harder. When government officials tell you that they can control money laundering, when they cannot even stop tons (many, many atoms) of cocaine and marijuana from crossing the border, it does not pass the laugh test.

To understand the problem the financial police face, one must consider the steps involved in monitoring potentially illegal transmissions. They first have to identify who might be sending money to whom. They then have to intercept the messages from the suspected parties, and then separate money instructions from normal communication—which is protected by the First Amendment. If the participants are encrypting their communication, then the government has to decide what to attempt to decrypt. Some encryption programs use a different key for each message sent—the "session key"—so the fact that you might have broken the code for one message does not mean that you can read subsequent messages between the same parties, even though they may be separated in time only by a matter of seconds. Remember, someone who "taps" into the message only intercepts a stream of 1s and 0s.

[33]Nicholas Negroponte, Being Digital (New York: Vintage Books, 1996), 14.

They have to figure out whose message it might be, and which stream of 1s and 0s might be important, and then try to break the code, which could take a huge amount of computing power.[34] It is hard to conceive how such attempts ever could be cost effective.

Now, knowing the above, if you are thinking this is a foolish thing for the government even to attempt to do, you are right. However, there are some government bureaucrats who do not care about cost effectiveness—after all, they are spending your money, not theirs. You can be sure that the folks at the Financial Crimes Enforcement Network (FinCEN), will come back and ask for even bigger budgets. They will claim they cannot do their job because their computers are not powerful enough, and that they need more personnel, and more authority to tap electronic messages. Their failure to do the impossible will not be used to shut down the activity, but will be used to justify a bigger budget. If you are unconvinced of this, you need only take a brief look at the expansion of the authority of both FinCEN and the Drug Enforcement Administration (DEA) to see how failure begets larger budgets. Almost no government ever willingly ends an activity until it absolutely must. People who believe they have an important mission will not be deterred because the mission is ever more difficult to achieve. Not only do they stand to lose their jobs, their power, and authority, but also their reason for being.

---

[34]Depending upon how the first message was broken, the intruders may be able to read the subsequent messages. For instance, if the private key of the receiver were stolen, then the passphrase guessed, all messages could be decoded. If the session key were somehow discovered, then subsequent messages could not be broken using that key. Probably the easiest way for a person to monitor your messages is to infiltrate your personal computer in some fashion and insert a short program to record all keystrokes over a certain period of time, monitoring those until you type your passphrase, then, lift your private key from your machine, and finally, tap into your e-mail to capture the encoded messages.

Liberation by Cryptography

*Past wars have been won or lost because the most
powerful governments on earth didn't have the
cryptological power any interested junior high school
student with a personal computer can harness today.
Soon any child old enough to use a computer
will be able to transmit encoded messages that
no government on earth will find easy to decipher.*

—Bill Gates[35]

Cryptography, the science of using mathematics to hide the meaning of messages, had been the almost exclusive domain of the US, French, Israeli, and Russian governments. Now, with the development of small, inexpensive, but powerful personal computers, and great advances in the science of cryptography, message security that is easy to use and almost unbreakable is available to everyone.

The process of disguising a message in order to hide its substance is called encryption. The encrypted message is called the ciphertext, which must be decrypted in order to be read. Cryptanalysis is the science of breaking the ciphertext. Cryptology is the branch of mathematics encompassing both cryptography and cryptanalysis.[36]

People have been encrypting messages for thousands of years. It is known that the ancient Egyptians used ciphers. Military commanders and diplomats have depended on en-

---

[35]Bill Gates, The Road Ahead (New York: Viking Penguin, 1995), 104.

[36]Readers desiring to obtain a more in-depth understanding of cryptography and related issues, including the mathematics, should refer to the almost encyclopedic Applied Cryptography: Protocols, Algorithms, and Source Code in C, by Bruce Schneier, published by John Wiley and Sons, Inc. 1996 or PGP: Pretty Good Privacy, by Simson Garfinkel, published by O'Reilly & Associates, Inc., 1995.

crypted messages to carry out their work for at least as long as history has been recorded. Most children have experimented with "secret codes," usually replacing one letter with another.

As new communications tools were developed, such as the telegraph and telephone, listening devices known as wiretaps were easily devised. Military commanders quickly understood the need for encrypting their own messages, and deciphering the encrypted messages of the enemy. The ability of the Allies to break both the Japanese and German codes—the Enigma machine—during WWII is credited with significantly shortening the war.

The creation of an unparalleled code-breaking capability became the highest order of importance for US intelligence agencies during the Cold War. One of the first uses of computers was to crack codes. In 1952, President Truman created the super-secret National Security Agency (NSA) to protect both US official and military communications, and to intercept and decode communications belonging to other governments. The NSA, headquartered at Fort Meade, Maryland, is reputed to have the world's greatest computer-processing capacity, and is the nation's biggest employer of mathematicians. It has been the chief government financial supporter of computer development. Having the world's biggest and best computers was a great selling tool for attracting the best mathematicians and new college graduates. For many years, the NSA had a well-deserved reputation for having the ability to crack any code. For better or worse, that is no longer true.

Unlike the Justice Department and the FBI, the NSA has been spared charges of politicization or corruption. By law, the NSA only has authority to listen to foreign citizens. Of course, these foreign citizens may be speaking with or exchanging data with an American citizen. The President, by Executive Order, can authorize an "NSA national security tap." These taps are supposedly limited to national security cases. Knowledgeable former government security officials, however, allege that the use of these "national security taps" has been greatly expanded under the Clinton Administration. Former National Security officials assert that some NSA officials have even refused to turn over material on American citizens to Administration officials, resisting what they believe to be attempts to politicize the organization.

The average American is probably unaware that most international telephone calls are intercepted, taped, and routed through NSA's computers. For example, if you are making a telephone call from Washington to Amsterdam, the call is routed by microwave to a place called Vint Hill Farms Station in Virginia. At that point it is intercepted by NSA, before it is sent by undersea cable or satellite to Europe. The computers are programmed to look for key words, for example, the name of a notorious Russian criminal. Calls containing key words or including targeted people are reviewed by NSA analysts. (The British, French, Israelis, and Russians are believed to operate in a similar manner).

The NSA data collection and analysis procedures work very well with "plain text." In this case, plain text is a normal unscrambled telephone call. However, NSA does have a problem with encrypted data because of both the volume of traffic, and the time and resources it takes to decrypt a targeted message once it is identified. There are literally billions of telephone calls and e-mail and other text messages being sent around the globe every day. Out of all of this "noise," the NSA must find the right phone call or data transmission, select the appropriate passages, and then attempt to decrypt them. It already is almost an impossible task.

Encryption in Your Future

*Cryptology represents the future of privacy, and more. By
implication, cryptology also represents the future of money,
and the future of banking and finance. ... Given the choice
between intersecting with a monetary system that leaves a
detailed electronic trail of one's financial activities, and a
parallel system that ensures anonymity and privacy, people
will opt for the latter. Moreover they will demand the latter,
because the current monetary system is being turned into the
principal instrument of surveillance and control by tyrannical
elements in Western governments.*

—J. Orlin Grabbe[37]

If you are not a foreign agent of an enemy power, a
terrorist, drug dealer, money launderer, kidnapper, tax evader,
or a member of an organized crime family, you may be
thinking, "I have no need for encryption." Now ask yourself,
would you mind if anyone who chose to make the effort, or
people at random, could listen to every phone conversation
you have, read every e-mail you send, read every document in
your computer, and see all of your financial records? Despite
being an upright and law-abiding citizen, you probably an-
swered "no" to the above—but, without encryption, all of your
communications and documents can be totally visible to anybody. Indeed, anyone who has been in a lawsuit knows—and
others can imagine—how innocent information can be twisted,
quotations misused, and ambiguities deployed in an insidious
manner.

Many sensitive documents are sent by e-mail, including
legal contracts, financial data, personnel evaluations, and business plans and proposals. Without encryption, all such information is subject to electronic eavesdropping. When you send

[37]J. Orlin Grabbe, "The End of Ordinary Money," Liberty (November 1995), 1.

an e-mail, the message is sent through many different computers, all of which can make a copy of it. Any computer operator anywhere along the line, and particularly at your e-mail server, can read or make a copy of it. Sending an e-mail message is not like sending a letter in a sealed envelope—it is like sending a post card. E-mail messages also may be delivered to the wrong party because of errors in any of the computers along the route—and this happens all too often.[38]

You need encryption to keep private documents and communications confidential. You also need encryption to make sure your documents are not modified without your consent. Finally, you need encryption to be certain that you are communicating with whom you think you are communicating and to verify electronic signatures for sensitive or legal documents.

Modern computer-based civilian encryption systems began in 1971 with an IBM developed private-key system known as "Lucifer." The code was designed to protect computer-based financial systems. The National Bureau of Standards (now NIST) developed and published in 1975 a standard for data encryption that could be used for both the storage and transmission of data, known as the Data Encryption Standard (DES). The DES algorithm uses a 56-bit key, which can easily be cracked by the NSA and by many commercial computers in a relatively short period of time. Despite the fact that DES can be foiled without too much difficulty, it is still in widespread use.

A major problem with DES, and any other private-key system, is that both the sender and receiver must agree on the encryption key. If someone eavesdrops or intercepts the key, the communication is not secure.

---

[38]Simson Garfinkel, PGP: Pretty Good Privacy (Sebastopol, CA: O'Reilly & Associates, Inc., 1995), 4-7.

The solution to the private key problem was the development of public key encryption. Two Stanford University researchers, Whitfield Diffie and Martin Hellman, wrote a paper in 1975 showing it was "possible to create a multi-user cryptography system in which a message could be encrypted with one key and decrypted with another."[39] Based on Diffie and Hellman's work, three MIT professors, Ronald Rivest, Adi Shamir, and Len Adleman, developed a public key encryption system in 1978, referred to as RSA. Whereas before, people wishing to exchange data had to share a key, which both encrypted and decrypted the messages, the RSA system implemented Diffie and Hellman's two-key encryption system—one key used to encrypt the message, and the other required to decrypt the message. Thus, RSA allowed for the widespread publication of the "encryption key" (or "public key"), which anyone could use to encrypt a message to send to the issuer of the said key. The issuer of the public key would keep the counterpart, his "private key," to himself. In this way, only the intended recipient would be able to decrypt a document, while anyone could send an encrypted message to this recipient.

These encryption systems are based on the fact that there is an infinite number of prime numbers. (A prime number is one that can only be divided evenly by 1 and itself, such as the numbers 2, 3, 5, 7, 11, 13, etc.) When you multiply two prime numbers together you get a number that can only be divided evenly by those same two prime numbers. While it is not difficult for a computer to multiply two large prime numbers, it is quite a bit more troublesome to reverse the process. That is, given the product of two large primes, it is difficult to figure out which two numbers were multiplied together to produce the given number. In general, the process of determining all of the numbers that evenly divide any other given number is

---

[39]Simson Garfinkel, PGP: Pretty Good Privacy (Sebastopol, CA: O'Reilly & Associates, Inc., 1995), 71-72.

known as factoring. There is no known easy, quick, and inexpensive way to factor very large numbers into their component prime numbers. Fast computers, using factoring software that employs the best known factoring algorithms, can be set to work to determine the component prime numbers. Even with these tools, it can still be a lengthy process. For example, it would take 100 million 8MB Pentium computers 14.5 seconds to crack a 429-bit key,[40] but it would take the same computers 280,000 years to crack a 1024-bit key.[41] The public key, which you can give to anyone, is the enciphering key which is based on the product of two prime numbers. The deciphering key, which you keep as your private key, is based on the prime numbers themselves. (Below is a footnote which explains how the RSA system works.[42])

Fortunately, you neither have to be a mathematician nor a

---

[40]Remember, a bit is a 1 or a 0, and all information to a computer is made up of streams of these bits. Therefore, a 429-bit key, is literally a number that, when written in binary form, is composed of a stream of 429 1s and 0s. In standard base 10, that would be a 129 digit number. Also note that 100 million computers is approximately equivalent to the number of personal computers that were sold in 1995.

[41]Simson Garfinkel, PGP: Pretty Good Privacy (O'Reilly & Associates, Inc., 1995), 360.

[42]For the mathematically adept and curious, the following is a description of how the RSA algorithm works, which is a modified version of the explanation given in PGP: Pretty Good Privacy on page 357.

Note: The mod function returns a remainder. For example, 7 mod 3 = 1. Some of you may recognize this as the equivalent of a finite number set. The mod function maps the first operand into the finite number set of the second operand.

Definitions:

p is a very large prime number

q is a second very large prime number

$n = p * q$ (n is the product of p and q)

e is a number which is relatively prime to the value $(p\text{-}1)*(q\text{-}1)$. e is the encryption key.

$d = e^{-1}(\text{mod}(p\text{-}1)*(q\text{-}1))$. d is the decryption key.

In order to derive d from e, one would have to know both p and q as well. The security depends on the numbers p and q never being revealed.

To perform the encryption, RSA takes the number to encrypt, which we will call m for message, and produces the ciphertext c according to the formula:

$c = m^e$ mod n

The decryption formula is:

$m = c^d$ mod n

Keep in mind that RSA works because there are no known easy methods to calculate d, p, or q given only n and e, which are the component parts of the public key. (It has not been rigorously proven that no easy methods of factoring exist. Nor is it absolutely proven that the only way to crack the algorithm is by factoring n into its component primes. But, this should not be of great concern, since mathematicians have been working on these problems for quite a while, and have yet to come up with any easy tricks to foil RSA.)

computer whiz to utilize public key encryption. There are programs that you can easily download into your personal computer and, with a few keystrokes, encrypt or decrypt e-mail or other documents, without having to understand the details of the process. One of the best known and most widely used of the near military grade encryption programs is PGP, which stands for Pretty Good Privacy. The program was originally developed in the early 1990s by Philip Zimmermann. It uses IDEA (*i.e.,* International Data Encryption Algorithm, developed in Switzerland by James L. Massey and Xuijia Lai, which uses a 128-bit key) for data encryption, and RSA (with keys up to 2047 bits) for key management and digital signatures. IDEA provides stronger encryption than the National Bureau of Standards' DES. PGP has a free version for personal use, which can be acquired via the Internet. Newer versions of PGP also use the DH/DSS key system.

The US government has made life difficult for many developers of public key encryption, and for Philip Zimmermann in particular, by claiming that electronic versions of encryption source code constitute "munitions," and hence are subject to export restrictions. An earlier version of PGP was placed on the Internet by someone and hence was available to anyone in the world, free of charge. Zimmermann was charged with violating US export restrictions but, after protracted litigation, the government dropped its suit. The courts have held that the First Amendment protects source code written on paper, even if it is exported. Given that any encryption program, including its source code, can be readily sent over the Internet, the attempt of governments to restrict exports or international usage of any particular system is both absurd and a total waste of taxpayer dollars. Negroponte explained this well:

> True, drug dealers, terrorists, and kiddie pornographers will use the Internet too. But

think about it. The bad guys are far better
equipped than you or I to outsmart the Feds
with encryption ... So, export laws and other
legislation are really foolish. If you ban the
export of encryption the only people who will
have it will be criminals. Far from protecting the
average citizen, this puts him at greater risk.
Lighten up, Washington.[43]

Digital signatures have become an important feature of
many encryption programs such as PGP. As electronic ways
of signing documents, digital signatures allow the receiver of
information to verify that a message actually was sent by the
person claiming to have sent it. The digital signature also
ensures that the message has not been changed since it was
signed. Indeed, if any transmission errors or deliberate tam-
pering have occurred, the digital signature will be rejected.
Digital signatures can be used to verify information or documents, including legal documents needing a time stamp.

For all practical purposes, virtually uncrackable public key
encryption is available at minimal cost to anyone who desires
to use it. PGP, utilizing a 1024-bit key, will adequately protect
almost anything that most people would wish to protect. At
some point, NSA or someone else will be able to crack
1024-bit keys in a reasonable period of time and without
excessive cost. When that time comes, users will merely need
to increase their key length. The longer the key, the more
secure the encryption, but the longer the key length the more
time it takes to encrypt and decrypt the message. If you are
only going to move $200 into your smart card, a key length of
4 digits (14 bits) is sufficient. If you are going to transfer a
million dollars, you would probably want to use at least a
128-bit key. Encryption, like any physical lock, should be

---

[43]Nicholas Negroponte, <u>Being Digital</u> (New York: Vintage Books, 1996), 235.

viewed as a method of delaying those who want to get into your safe. It is never permanent for all time. In the real world the cost to the government or anyone else to pick these electronic locks will not be worth the effort if users are careful to use strong enough encryption to insure that the cost of acquiring the information is greater than the value of the information acquired.

Chapter IV

THE ASSAULT ON
FINANCIAL PRIVACY

*Next to the right of liberty, the right of property is the
most important individual right guaranteed by the
Constitution and the one which, united with that of
personal liberty, has contributed more to the growth
of civilization than any other institution established
by the human race.*

—William Howard Taft

Laws that Permit Intrusive Government

D id you know that every time you write a check, or use
a credit or debit card, the details of that transaction
are kept, and can be accessed by employees of the US
government, in addition to your bank? The average American
is unaware of how completely his financial privacy has already
been stripped away by a series of laws and regulations whose

avowed purpose is to capture tax evaders, drug dealers, money launderers, and assorted criminals.

The Bank Secrecy Act is, in fact, a bank anti-secrecy act, because it requires that your bank transactions *not* be secret. Your friendly neighborhood banker is required to spy on you, while you pay him. In fact, if your banker *does not* spy on you, he will be subject to criminal prosecution and fines. In a news story, one learns that "American Express was fined $7 million for failing to detect money-laundering, and agreed to forfeit to the US Justice Department another $7 million."[44] Most Americans were justifiably outraged when, after the fall of the Berlin Wall, they learned how the German secret police, the "Stasi," required neighbors to spy on each other. Yet what the US government is asking of bankers is similar in nature if not in degree or motivation.

The President's Commission on Organized Crime has defined money laundering as the "process by which one conceals the existence, illegal source, or illegal application of income, and then disguises that income to make it appear legitimate."[45] This definition lacks precision but can be made endlessly expansive. Is the act of taking and reporting political donations from Buddhist Nuns, who were given the money by someone else, money laundering? The law is sufficiently vague to make selective enforcement inevitable. (Selective enforcement is a problem with many laws, but as a general rule it is best to avoid laws that, by their basic construct, lend themselves to such abuse). If you are a friend or political crony of the prosecutor, no charge. If you are on the wrong side of the political fence or a critic of the prosecutor, you are unlikely to receive any mercy. The nature of tyranny, as Hitler and Stalin showed, is to pass so many laws as to make everyone a potential criminal, and actual law enforcement

[44] J. Orlin Grabbe, "The Money Laundromat," Liberty, November 1995, 33.
[45] Ibid.

effectively arbitrary. It is ironic that officials of the Clinton Administration complained about many of the tactics that Independent Counsel Kenneth Starr used against them, while at the same time advocated giving federal prosecutors more authority to be used against ordinary citizens.

In order to make all of these regulations and requirements more comprehensible to the poor bankers and tellers, The Treasury Department's Office of the Comptroller of the Currency (OCC) has published a pamphlet entitled, "Money Laundering: A Banker's Guide to Avoiding Problems." According to the government guide:

> The US has imposed many legislative and regulatory standards to deter money laundering. The most significant of these are:
> - The Bank Secrecy Act of 1970
> - The Money Laundering Control Act of 1986
> - The Anti-Drug Abuse Act of 1988
> - Section 2532 of the Crime Control Act of 1990
> - Section 206 of the Federal Deposit Insurance Corporation Improvement Act of 1991
> - Title XV of the Housing and Community Development Act of 1992
>
> The statute makes it illegal for a financial institution or employee to disclose, to the subject of a referral or a grand jury subpoena, that a criminal referral has been filed or a grand jury investigation has been initiated in connection with a possible crime involving a violation of money laundering and BSA laws. Officers who improperly disclose information concerning grand jury subpoena for bank records are subject to prosecution.[46]

In addition to the above-mentioned laws, there is the Annunzio-Wylie Anti-Money Laundering Act of 1992, and the Money Laundering Suppression Act of 1994. Quite obviously, no one can know all of the provisions and interpretations of all of these acts and derivative regulations.

In order to detect money laundering, banks have been charged with the responsibility of detecting and reporting any suspicious activity to the US government. The Office of the Comptroller of the Currency provides banks with very detailed and lengthy lists of suspicious activities. For example, the OCC suggests to be aware of:

- A customer who often visits the safety box area immediately before making cash deposits just under a reportable threshold.
- An account or customer that has frequent deposits of musty or extremely dirty bills.
- A customer who suddenly pays down a large problem loan with no reasonable explanation of the source of the funds.
- A customer whose home phone is disconnected.
- A customer who has no record of past or present employment but makes frequent large transactions.
- A business that is reluctant to reveal details about its activities or to provide financial statements.
- A business that presents financial statements noticeably different from those of similar businesses.

---

[46]This text is from the Treasury Department's Office of the Comptroller of the Currency's web site, at http://www.occ.treas.gov/launderer/orig1.html, from the pamphlet, "Money Laundering: A Banker's Guide to Avoiding Problems."

Further, they caution to make note of the following unusual characteristics or activities:

- ◆ Unusual cash purchases of money orders
  and cashier's checks.
- ◆ A single, substantial cash deposit composed
  of many $50 and $100 bills.
- ◆ Frequent exchanges of small bills for large
  bills or vice versa.
- ◆ An account that shows several deposits below a specified threshold made at automatic
  teller machines.
- ◆ Wiring cash or proceeds of a cash deposit to
  another country without changing the form
  of currency.

Even bank employees should be watched by their managers, and thus they should be on the lookout for (among
other things):

- ◆ An employee whose lavish lifestyle cannot
  be supported by his or her salary.
- ◆ An employee who is reluctant to take a
  vacation.

Obviously, there are some criminals who fit these criteria,
but almost everyone at some time in his life will do some of
the things that will land him on the suspicious lists. If it is you,
your bank, in order to protect itself, will file a report on you.
Since April 1996, US banks have been required to provide the
government with more suspicious activity reports. More than
114,000 of these reports were filed in the first eight months.
Money laundering might not be well defined, but if federal
prosecutors want to get you, they will. "In 1993, a federal
judge in Providence, Rhode Island issued the longest sentence
ever given to a nonviolent legal offense: 600 years in prison for

money laundering. The launderer had been fingered by his bankers, who then cooperated in building a case against him..."[47]

Bad Laws in Bad Hands

When I set up the Asset Forfeiture Office, I thought I could use my position to help protect citizens' rights, and tried to ensure that the US Department of Justice went after big drug dealers and big time criminals, rather than minor offenders and innocent property owners. Today, overzealous government agents and prosecutors will not think twice about seizing a yacht or car if they find two marijuana cigarettes in it, regardless of where they came from. I am now ashamed of, and scared of, the monster I helped to create.

–Judge John Yoder[48]

You have to wonder how law schools admit intelligent people, with some moral compass, who are able to read and write in English, and then graduate people who can no longer tell right from wrong, or read and understand the straightforward language in the US Constitution. For instance, except for federal judges, most people understand that the present money laundering laws violate the Fourth Amendment (searching and seizing papers without a warrant), and the Fifth Amendment (protection against self-incrimination).[49]

---

[47]J.Orlin Grabbe, "The Money Laundromat," Liberty, November 1995, 32.

[48]Judge Yoder was the first Director of the Asset Forfeiture Office at the US Department of Justice, former state district court judge, and former state senator.

[49]A number of lawyers will argue that these Amendments do not apply to civil proceedings. Agencies routinely get around the requirements of these Amendments by pursuing information under the guise of civil proceedings, then, upon gathering sufficient information, transfer this information to make a criminal case against their victim. Also, although it is well-established in law that just compensation is due to those who have produced work, businesses (i.e., banks) are routinely required to produce work for an entity (i.e., the government) without any compensation at all. This may not constitute slavery as would be prohibited under the Thirteenth Amendment, but it is certainly unjust.

A police state does not announce itself. Its progenitors may not even intend it. It comes in the slow and ceaseless erosion of liberties and privacy, all in the name of doing good. In 1997, the Department of the Treasury promulgated 59 pages of proposed regulations, mind-boggling in complexity, to greatly expand its ability to monitor and regulate how and where you spend your money. Specifically, the regulations require registration and reporting by "money services businesses," which are defined as businesses that provide check cashing, currency exchange, money orders, or stored value (*i.e.*, "smart cards"), and sellers or redeemers of travelers checks, or other similar instruments, in amounts as little as $500 per day per person. Obviously, most businesses could end up falling under such expansive definitions. In addition, the regulations require "money transmitters and their agents to report and retain records of transactions in currency or monetary instruments of at least $750 in connection with the transmission or other transfer of funds to any person outside the United States, and to verify the identity of senders of such transmissions or transfers."

In other words, the US government is demanding to know where you send much of your money. Why is this being done? The claim is that the government needs these enhanced powers to combat drug and other illegal money laundering. The previous regulations applied mainly to banks, and generally had reporting thresholds from $3,000 to $10,000. These too were put in place to combat the criminals, but clearly had not worked. Thus, the call for more far-reaching and costly regulations.

As a trial run, the Treasury Department imposed an Order on the geographic region of New York on a temporary basis, which implemented regulations on transactions destined for Colombia. During the period of study, transfers to Colombia dropped approximately thirty percent. Obviously, some of the drop reflects a number of criminals discouraged from sending illegally-gained funds directly to Colombia. But part of this drop can no doubt be attributed to legitimate wire transferors who were wary of placing their family or friends on lists of suspects, and causing them potential legal difficulties. The study also proved that criminals will look for and find ways to avoid detection, even with the regulations in place. Once the Order was in effect, the number of transmissions under the $750 reporting threshold doubled, and the FinCEN report also surmised "that launderers are now moving large sums through other money transmitters in other cities."

The Order was put in effect in August 1996, and expired in June 1997. The study reports that, in this time, twenty-two search warrants were served, five people were indicted, and there were three arrest warrants outstanding. After a great deal of time and money spent by the regulators, and at the expense of the privacy of many legitimate wire transferors, five arrests were made. Was it worth it?

These new proposed regulations, as extensive and oppressive as they are, are still littered with loopholes that any reasonably competent Mafia boss or drug kingpin will easily be able to walk through. You can then be assured that the Treasury Department will come back and say that the $750 limit is still too high, and they need to know everything about every expenditure. In the day of electronic commerce, the government will need to know everything or it will only know what people want it to know. As bad as drug gangs and Mafia types are, it is doubtful that Americans are willing to give up all of their financial privacy to make only a small dent in criminal activity. No CEO of a public company could accept the poor performance or rate of return routinely endured by the Treasury and FinCEN.

Reading the proposed regulations and definitions, it is

unclear exactly who will be required to report. Hundreds of thousands, if not millions, of American businesses and individuals will be affected. The Treasury acknowledges that the regulations will cost tens of millions of dollars, and its estimates are likely to be greatly understated. The Treasury assumes that the regulations will be clear and understandable to the average person—an assumption not supported by the proposals. They also assume that the correct forms will always be available and that people will be able to get speedy, clear, and correct answers to their questions from government—but the publicized actions of the IRS give rise to great doubt to this assumption too. Ordinary people will be confused and confounded.

But now that the new regulations have been enacted, professional money launderers will quickly change their ways of doing things in order not to be caught. It is unlikely that they will say to themselves, "Hey, money laundering is now more difficult and costly, so I will give up pushing drugs." If drug dealers are able to import drugs without being detected, how likely is it that they will find it more difficult to send money back through the same channels? The new hundred and fifty dollar bills contain metallic threads, which may be possible to detect through magnetic scanners.[50] The Treasury Department has considered this in the design of the new currency. Still, those who are savvy and determined will find ways to get around the new obstacles to money laundering.

The officials in the Federal government who are advocating all of these draconian regulations will tell us that they are doing it for our own good in order to protect us. Indeed, a few witless or careless criminals may be caught by the new regulations. But the most professional ones will not, while the regulations will increase costs to the general public and reduce

---

[50]These metallic threads will also be added to the rest of the currency as it is updated.

people's privacy. Indeed, some federal officials seem to have the attitude that it would be better to lose all financial privacy than to let one criminal go free. As a result of these regulations, the government will be deluged with millions of pieces of very confidential information. Who is going to see this material? Officials at the Treasury and Justice Departments will tell us that adequate safeguards will be put in place to protect our privacy. Their assurance is not credible. These are the same people who are sworn to protect our income tax and FBI records, and we know what all too often has happened with them.

Just imagine the damage that could be done if the financial data the government is proposing to collect falls into the wrong hands, as some of it almost certainly will. The US government frequently shares sensitive data with foreign governments, particularly in relation to the war on drugs. Also, foreign governments will have an incentive to place individuals sensitive to their concerns (i.e., spies) in the Treasury Department's financial reporting structure. For example, a Treasury employee with pro-Palestinian terrorist leanings might pass on information about contributors to Israeli causes, making them targets. Americans contributing to pro-democracy or pro-environmental movements in authoritarian countries could endanger the lives of the recipients, if their financial data were leaked or stolen. Religious groups contributing to missionary movements in repressive countries might see their converts and workers repressed or their lives put in danger. Thousands of relatives of Americans or legal foreign nationals living overseas and receiving legitimate funds could be the victims of criminals or foreign government agents, if the amounts of the received funds were known.

In domestic trials of controversial persons, private financial information may become subject to insider leaks to the media. The one thing you know is that when a government official tells you that your financial privacy will be protected and abuse will not happen, he or she cannot make such categorical claims. Thousands upon thousands of people will have access to your private financial dealings, and there is no way to know that all of them will be honorable. Government employees are no more or less virtuous than the rest of us, which means that some of them will take advantage if given the chance.[51] Some may nurture political grievances or agendas. Unfortunately, the US government has a long history of abuse of citizens' rights. We know that Kennedy, Johnson, Nixon and Clinton all misused sensitive information. If this will happen outside the law, imagine what might occur if the law tends to justify massive snooping. "Bad laws," Burke reminds us, "are the worst sort of tyranny."

The Abuse of Asset Forfeiture

No greater erosion of basic rights for Americans, and particularly the right to property, has occurred than from the abuse of asset forfeiture laws since 1970. Federal, state, and local authorities routinely seize the assets of suspected drug dealers, tax evaders and others, without warrants charging them with a crime, or due process. If your property is seized, you must sue to get it back and prove that it was taken unlawfully. If you win in court, as a high percentage of those who have had their property seized do, you will not be able to collect the legal fees incurred nor be compensated for any damage to your property while it was in the custody of government officials. Seized property is often sold, and the proceeds are placed in the budgets of the government agents or agencies that seized it.

---

[51]The Washington Post reported on May 1, 1998 that, "A rogue Internal Revenue Service agent tried to frame former Senate Majority leader Howard H. Baker, Jr. on money laundering and bribery charges in a bizarre attempt by the agent to advance his career ..." Even if you are rich, famous, or powerful, you may still be subject to such abuse.

Such activity by agents of the government is clearly prohibited by the Constitution, by both the Fifth Amendment, which states that private property shall not "be taken for public use without just compensation," and the Fourteenth Amendment, which states "nor shall any State deprive any person of life, liberty, or property, without due process of law." The <u>Wall Street Journal</u> published a letter to the editor, which cited the long-standing distaste for asset forfeiture law. In it, Donald J. Boudreaux, of the Foundation for Economic Education wrote:

> James Wilson of Pennsylvania, one of the most influential members of the 1787 Constitutional Convention, despised the fact that under forfeiture statutes "an insult to society becomes a pecuniary favor to the crown." Wilson also understood that, with forfeiture, "the appointed guardian of the publick security becomes interested in the violation of the law; and the hallowed ministers of justice become the rapacious agents of the treasury." Perhaps our Supreme Court justices should study the Founders' thoughts on forfeiture.[52]

Despite the obvious violation of Constitutional protections, many courts have upheld such seizures. Such cases show that all too many judges have come to believe in the rule of men rather than law. Judge Yoder, the first Director of the Asset Forfeiture Office at the US Department of Justice, appalled at the current practices of asset forfeiture, writes:

> I always saw the danger of asset forfeiture when I set up the Asset Forfeiture Office at the U.S. Department of Justice in 1983, but never, in my wildest imagination, did I think it would

---

[52]Donald J. Boudreaux, "Forfeiture Statutes 'An Insult to Society,'" <u>Wall Street Journal</u>. 20 Jan. 1998, A19.

be used to abuse liberty and property rights so quickly, and with so little resistance from the legislative branch, the federal courts, and the public. None of them apparently saw the dangers that our founding fathers saw when they put the Bill of Rights in the United States Constitution.

Now, fifteen years later, the abuses of the government in forfeiting assets is totally out of control. It goes to show that in the name of a good cause, government tyranny and abuse can slip into place almost overnight with the full support of the people, and become an acceptable practice, with few questions asked.

If the government agents find a trace of marijuana in a car, or yacht, or house, they can seize the property, regardless of the innocence of the owner. And, unlike the criminal laws, asset forfeiture laws are civil, and there is no presumption of innocence. The property is presumed to be guilty until proven innocent, and there is no requirement that guilt be proved beyond a reasonable doubt.

Even when I oversaw the asset forfeiture initiative at the U.S. Department of Justice 15 years ago, DEA agents did not necessarily decide to seize a car based on how bad a criminal was, but based on which cars they wanted to drive. For example, if a DEA agent saw a Rolls Royce or a Mercedes or a BMW he wanted to drive, he would check to see if it had a loan on it. If it had a loan on it, the agent would not seize it, because the loan would have to be paid off by the government before the agent could drive it and use it. This has got to be one of the worst abuses of government power and corruption, where a government agent can seize a car from a citizen, and then use it for his or her own transportation. Of course, the big criminals quickly figured this out, so they leased their cars. Now, a DEA agent is more likely to seize the Mercedes of a legitimate businessman who has paid for the car, but whose teenage son smoked a marijuana cigarette in the car without the knowledge of his father, than to seize the car of a real drug dealer.[53]

The abuse of asset forfeiture has become so widespread and outrageous that a few public officials are trying to take some limited corrective action. No one has been more outspoken on the need for a return to Constitutional protections than the highly regarded Chairman of the House Judiciary Committee, Congressman Henry Hyde. In his book, Forfeiting Our Property Rights, Congressman Hyde explains the origins of these asset forfeiture laws:

> Impelled by the exigencies of the so-called war on drugs, the broadly written Racketeer Influenced and Corrupt Organizations Act (RICO), and subsequent amendments to federal anti-drug laws, the hoary doctrines of Anglo-American civil asset forfeiture law have been resurrected, like some jurisprudential Franken-stein monster, from the dark recesses of past centuries. (If that sounds alarmingly scary, it is meant to be.) And like Mary Shelley's well-meaning fictional doctor who gave life to the

---

[53]John Yoder, e-mail to the author, 10 March 1998.

mindless monster, eager federal and state legislators, and their often unquestioning judicial ac-
complices, seem loath to recognize the extent of
the consequent destruction of our constitutional
rights and basic liberties.[54]

The asset forfeiture laws are so sweeping that they imperil
the rights and liberties of all of us. Congressman Hyde further
warns:

> Much of what you may have learned in
> school or college about your rights and liberties
> no longer applies. Increased government and
> police powers, rising criminal activity and vio-
> lence, popular anxiety about drug use—all have
> become justifications for curtailing the applica-
> tion of the Bill of Rights and the individual
> security it once guaranteed. Federal and state
> officials now have the power to seize your busi-
> ness, home bank account, records, and personal
> property, all without indictment, hearing, or
> trial. Everything you have can be taken away at
> the whim of one or two federal or state officials
> operating in secret. Regardless of sex, age, race,
> or economic station, we are all potential victims.
> And unless these trends are recognized and
> reversed, there will soon be very little that indi-
> viduals can do to protect their property or them-
> selves.[55]

Almost daily, in newspapers or magazines, one can find
examples of government officials abusing the forfeiture law. In
their zeal to grab other people's property, government authori-

---

[54]Henry Hyde, Forfeiting Our Property Rights: Is Your Property Safe From Seizure?
(Washington, DC: Cato Institute, 1995), 1.
    [55]Ibid., 2.

ties use the pretext of minor mistakes in the endless forms
citizens are forced to fill out in order to seize assets or impose
outrageous fines. Travelers who carry more than $10,000
into or out of the US must fill out Form 4790. Failure to
do so can lead to the seizure of the funds by Customs
officials. The fact that the money is honest and hard-
earned is "not relevant," according to the Customs Service.[56] Note—it is not illegal to transport more than
$10,000. What is illegal is the failure to fill out the form, even
if there are no forms available—which is a common occur-
rence.[57]

Asset forfeiture is applied on a very selective basis—all
citizens are not equal under the law when it comes to who is
targeted. Authorities tend to go after those who have visible,
readily seizable, and salable assets—planes, boats, expensive
real estate, and cars. If you are rich and unpopular with the
ruling group or media, because of your political views or for
other reasons, you may be a target. Foreigners are another
favorite target, because they often do not know how to protect
themselves. Also, those foreigners who come from countries
where there is extensive drug dealing are often considered
guilty just because of their citizenship, not because of any
wrongdoing on their part.

A Venezuelan citizen who operated duty-free shops
throughout the Caribbean, including stores in Colombia,
had his account in a Miami bank frozen by US government agents. He had not committed any crime, but the Feds
froze his account on the pretext that he made payments in
Colombia (which were part of this legitimate business). He
sued to get his money back and was eventually vindicated,

---

[56]James Bovard, "Crimes on Paper," American Spectator, January 1998, 44.
[57]Readers interested in obtaining details of recent governmental abuse of citizens rights in the
US should read the superb book by James Bovard, Lost Rights: The Destruction of American
Liberty.

but was not compensated for the considerable financial loss he incurred to get his money back.[58]

Similarly, a Colombian property developer having legitimate business operations in the US had $10,000,000 in an Atlanta bank frozen by government officials. He went to court and got his money back. He then moved the deposit from Atlanta to a Miami bank, where the money was again frozen. He went to court again and got his money back. Each of these court proceedings cost him a considerable amount.[59]

Again, an elderly Colombian couple who had been operating a shoe business in Colombia had been sending small amounts of money to a Miami bank for many years. They had planned to retire in Miami because their children lived there. The Feds froze their money with a totally unsubstantiated and false claim that they were running a money laundering business.[60]

Judge Yoder explains the lengths to which officials will go for convictions in their cases, far beyond what could be considered reasonable:

> Today, the asset forfeiture laws are also more likely to be used to intimidate someone who is innocent, than to go after someone who is a big time criminal or drug dealer. For example, in 1993, I was appointed by a federal judge to represent a Jamaican who was accused of selling 1.3 grams of crack on a first-time offense. As I was preparing for trial, I listed the employer as a character witness for my client, and sent the employer's name and address to

---

[58]Norman Bailey, interview by author, 12 December 1997.
[59]Ibid.
[60]Ibid.

the federal judge and U.S. Attorney's Office as required to do by law.

The day after the U.S. Attorney's Office saw the employer listed as a witness, the government sent him a letter clearly meant to intimidate him into not testifying at trial. The employer was a land-owner, and the Assistant U.S. Attorney prosecuting the case threatened to seize one of the rental apartment houses he owned because they were suspicious that some tenants in one of the rental units were using drugs. Clearly, this heavy-handed threat of seizing his land and property were designed to intimidate him into not testifying in the case. If an ordinary person used these kind of threats and tactics to intimidate someone into not testifying in a case, they would be charged with obstruction and sent to prison, but in the name of fighting drugs, anything seems to be fair game anymore as far as federal and state prosecutors are concerned. I believe that their new motto is: "The citizens' rights be damned—we are above the law because we work for the government."[61]

With such sweeping power and haphazard use, the asset forfeiture laws are akin to government theft. Congressman Hyde also notes in his book the moral wrong committed by the state against its citizens as a result of civil asset forfeiture:

The right to ownership of property is implicit in the Seventh Commandment, "Thou shalt not steal." Those who distinguish between property rights and "human rights" commit a

---

[61]John Yoder, e-mail to the author, 10 March 1998.

fundamental error—property rights are human rights, among the most important of all human rights. To exist and prosper, every human being needs material goods—property. A person cannot live without the means to support life. We all have the right to supply our needs by using what we own—our "Lives, Liberties, and Estates," as John Locke put it-free from disturbance by others. I believe, as did St. Thomas Aquinas, and Aristotle before him, that the natural law recognizes in every person the right to property.[62]

America the Financial Imperialist

America is a large friendly dog in a very small room. Every time it wags its tail it knocks over a chair.

—Arnold Toynbee

If something is illegal in America, many Americans think it ought to be illegal everywhere. And likewise, if something is legal in America, Americans think it ought to be legal everywhere.[63] The problem with this worldview is that it is not shared by much of the rest of the world.

American law is largely an outgrowth of the English common law, and hence most of those countries that England once ruled have a somewhat similar approach to the law. Much of

---

[62]Henry Hyde, Forfeiting Our Property Rights: Is Your Property Safe From Seizure? (Washington, DC: Cato Institute, 1995), 3.

[63]Governments also occasionally have one set of standards for their citizens, and a different set for foreigners, when it is to their advantage to do so. For example, it is illegal for Russian citizens to acquire real estate abroad or to open a bank account abroad without first obtaining a permit from the Central Bank of Russia (which for all intents and purposes is nearly impossible), while at the same time the Russians are encouraging foreign citizens to invest in and open bank accounts in Russia.

continental Europe, on the other hand, has a legal system derived from the Napoleonic code. Many of the Moslem countries have systems based on Islamic law, which, for example, prohibits the payment of interest.

While all societies have strict rules against murder and theft, there are activities which are serious crimes in some countries but not in others. Many environmental crimes are unknown in the former communist countries and the Third World. Whether prostitution, pot smoking, adultery, public nudity at the beach, and slander are crimes depends on where you are. The same is true with financial crimes. For example, there are very different attitudes among societies towards tax evasion, money laundering, bribe-taking, and nepotism.

Most countries have a territorial system of taxation, whereby a person only pays tax on the money earned in that particular country. The US has a worldwide tax system, in which citizens and permanent US residents are taxed on their worldwide income. Most countries do not have a capital gains tax, at least not a broad one like the US.

These real differences cause serious conflict. This is particularly true when the US tries to apply its laws outside the territory of the US—especially when the activity is not illegal in the foreign country.

US authorities often inspect people's bank accounts wherever the account might be, and in fact, some US officials at times even have tried to look in foreign bank accounts of non-US citizens. Many countries look at such behavior as unseemly and immoral. A number of countries have passed real bank privacy laws, unlike the US Bank (anti) Secrecy Act, to prohibit private bank officials and government officials from looking into private bank accounts. In contrast, US officials have been known to pressure foreign governments and bankers to look at private accounts. These requests often generate considerable friction, particularly when the IRS or FBI demands that foreign officials violate their own laws. For example, Swiss bank privacy does not apply to accounts where the money is believed to have come from criminal sources. However, tax avoidance is not considered a criminal offense in Switzerland, and hence the veil of bank privacy will not be removed for the IRS.

US bank regulatory authorities are very insistent on requiring banks to "know their customers." This regulation is imposed on foreign banks doing business in the US as well as US banks operating in foreign countries, and the regulation is not just limited to these banks' accounts in the United States. Many people like to hold their bank accounts in the name of a separate entity for privacy and protection. It is common for wealthy South Americans to set up bank accounts in offshore branches of large international banks in the name of their personal investment company, rather than their own name, as a shield against kidnapping. In order to protect their citizens, a number of South American countries make it illegal for a bank to reveal the name of the beneficial owner. But US authorities often demand to know the real owners of these accounts. The international banks are then put in the impossible situation of being unable to comply with the conflicting laws of two different countries.

According to US law, foreign banks operating in the United States are supposed to be treated by the regulatory authorities exactly the same as the US banks, yet bank executives of foreign banks operating in the US find that this is not always the case. Some US government regulatory officials are so uninformed that they assume that anyone who has an account in a foreign bank—particularly a bank whose home country has bank privacy laws, such as Switzerland—must be engaged in criminal activities, and as a result, treat responsible and highly professional bank executives working for foreign banks as if they worked for dishonorable organizations. It appears never to have occurred to these US officials that Americans and others might wish to have accounts in foreign-owned banks because they get better or a wider range of services than they get from US-owned banks.[64]

Most Americans, and especially American business people, like the fact that US banks operate in many foreign countries. It serves their American customers well. If Americans want US banks to have the right to operate in foreign countries and not be discriminated against, then they need to extend the same privileges and courtesies to foreign-owned banks operating in the US.

There are endless examples of abusive and improper behavior by US officials against foreign bankers and citizens. For instance, the Journal of Commerce notes that, "In a case involving Marine Midland Bank, prosecutors froze $7 million in the correspondent account of the Hong Kong and Shanghai Bank in Panama, even though they were only looking for $1.5 million in dirty money." In another example:

> Bank Leu SA of Luxembourg forfeited $2.3 million to the US government and more than $1 million to Luxembourg following a money-laundering guilty plea in San Francisco, even though Bank Leu had no branch in the United States. The charge? Clearing US dollars drawn on a US bank but deposited by non-US citizens in Luxembourg.[65]

If any foreign country had treated US citizens and banks in a

---

[64]Examples of such behavior were given to me by senior officers of Swiss banks operating in the United States. For obvious reasons, they have chosen to remain anonymous.

[65]"Clean Getaway for Money Launderers," Journal of Commerce, 10 December 1996, 63.

similar manner, there would have been screams of outrage. US politicians and authorities would have demanded sanctions. This hypocrisy blemishes the reputation of the United States.

Excessive Costs of Compliance with Worthless Regulations

The regulations and reporting requirements imposed by the US government on financial institutions are not only a violation of Americans' civil liberties, but fail the most elementary tests of costs and benefits. Senior bank compliance executives estimate that approximately 15 - 20% of bank operating costs in the US are due to the costs of trying to comply with federal money laws and regulations.[66] The reason

---

[66]In an attempt to rein in the costs of federal regulations, Congressman Ron Paul submitted his dissenting view regarding money laundering bills H.R. 4005, the Money Laundering Deterrence Act of 1998, and H.R. 1756, the Money Laundering and Financial Crimes Strategy Act of 1998. In it he says:

> The costs of showing that one complies with the current forms far exceed any alleged benefit. These bills will only add to that burden. Calculations using statistics provided by the Financial Crimes Enforcement Network (FinCEN) put costs of compliance at $83,454,000 in 1996 for just one law, the Bank Secrecy Act. This estimate was made by totaling only the number of forms required by the Bank Secrecy Act (multiplied by the cost of compliance of each type of form) to the respondent financial institution, according to numbers supplied in response to a September 1997 request by my office to FinCEN. Two forms were not included in the total which undoubtedly would push the current total compliance cost higher: IRS 8852 had been required for less than one year, and TDF 90-2249 was not yet active...

> Compliance costs for smaller banks are disproportionately high. According to a study prepared for the Independent Bankers Association of America by Grant Thorton in 1993, annual compliance costs for the Bank Secrecy Act in 1992 were estimated at 2,083,003 hours and $59,660,479 just for community banks. It noted that "smaller banks face the highest compliance cost in relation to total assets, equity capital and net income before taxes. For each $1 million in assets, banks less than $30 million in assets incur almost three times the compliance cost of banks between $30 - 65 million in assets. These findings are consistent for both equity capital and net income measurements." In short, these regulations impose a marginal advantage to larger institutions and are a contributing factor to the rise in mergers into ever-larger institutions. These bills will only exacerbate this factor...

> *The Cost of Banking Regulation: A Review of the Evidence,* (Gregory Elliehausen, Board of Governors of the Federal Reserve System Staff Study 171, April 1998), concurs that the new regulations will impose a disproportionately large cost on smaller institutions. The estimated aggregate cost of bank regulation (non-interest expenses) on commercial banks was $125.9 billion in 1991, according to the Fed Staff Study. As the introduction of new entrants into the market becomes more costly, smaller institutions will face a marginally increased burden and will be more likely to consolidate. "The basic conclusion is similar for all of the studies of economies of scale: Average compliance costs for regulations are substantially greater for banks at low levels of

the cost is so high is that almost all bank employees have to be trained and monitored to make sure they are adequately spying on their customers. Each transaction has to be evaluated, and any transaction involving large amounts of money or cash in excess of $3,000 must be reported.

Government does not make the task any easier. The forms that are submitted to the government must be typed, even though most banks no longer use typewriters, but computers. The bank compliance officer of one of the world's largest banks said that when he asked if they could supply the reports in electronic format, he was given the software for the forms from the bank regulators. However, when he tried to submit the reports using the software he had been given by the government, he was told that the regulations still required him to submit individual typed reports.[67]

These costs are, of course, passed on to the banks' customers. In essence, Americans are paying billions of dollars each year in hidden federal taxes on their financial operations. What do they get for this "tax," besides a massive invasion into their financial privacy? Not much![68]

In the ten-year period from 1987-1996, banks filed more

---

output than for banks at moderate or high levels of output," the Staff study concludes.

"The drive to stem these flows has imposed an enormous paperwork burden on banks. According to the American Bankers Association, the cost of meeting all the regulations required by the US government may total $10 billion a year. That might be acceptable if convictions for money laundering kept pace with the millions of documents banks must file each year. But the scorecard has been disappointing," reads the Journal of Commerce (December 10, 1996).

[67]from an anonymous interview with a Senior bank compliance executive for a major world bank, January 1998.

[68]This invasion of financial privacy is not trivial. Congressman Ron Paul also notes that: "The mere existence of the databases holding confidential information on private individuals opens up the possibility of abuse. Unfortunately, it is not just an unfounded fear based on hypotheticals. In fact, the employees of FinCEN itself cannot always be trusted. In 1993, one employee took the liberty of using the resources at his disposal to do a little digging into the (assumed to be) private records of the mother of his girlfriend. In the same year, another employee of FinCEN left her desk unattended with the opportunity available for others to access privileged information—and someone else used the opportunity to pursue personally-motivated independent research."

THE ASSAULT ON FINANCIAL PRIVACY

than 77 million Currency Transactions Reports (CTRs) with the US Treasury. This amounts to approximately 308,000 pounds of paper.[69] Such reports caused the government to file about 3,000 money laundering cases between 1987 and 1995. 7,300 defendants were charged but only 580 people were convicted, according to the Justice Department.[70] Environmentalists take note: this works out to about 531 pounds of paper per conviction.

The government often runs sting operations in luxurious Caribbean locations. Such operations are great for scenes in movies, but in reality most of them are a big waste of tax money.[71] Of the 290 people charged as a result of the bank sting operations between 1990 and 1995, only 29 were found guilty.[72] The real tragedy is the cost to all of those innocent people who had huge legal expenses and/or their lives ruined because of incompetent and, in some cases, over-zealous government prosecutors.

There is no evidence that the government anti-money laundering crusade has had any appreciable impact on drug dealing, terrorism or organized crime. The few convictions that have been obtained are in almost all cases the "small fry."

---

[69]Former Federal Reserve Governor Lawrence Lindsey, Cato Institute Debate, "Should Money Laundering Be a Crime?" Cato Institute, Washington, DC 5 December 1997.

[70]"Clean Getaway for Money Launderers," Journal of Commerce, 10 December 1996, 62.

[71]Not only are these stings a financial bust, but occasionally they damage US relations with foreign countries. Congressman Ron Paul cites the example of what happened in Mexico after the Operation Casablanca sting:

The police 'sting' operation has caused international problems since such operations are illegal in Mexico with some referring to it as 'a debacle for U.S. diplomacy.' Rosario Green, Mexico's foreign minister, says, 'This has been a very strong blow to binational cooperation, especially on matters of drug trafficking.' (Wall Street Journal, May 28, 1998) U.S. banks named in the investigation were left untouched. She claims to have evidence that U.S. agents broke Mexican law and Mexico may demand their extradition; she termed the operation a 'violation of national sovereignty.'

The illegal sting operation will make only a paltry dent in money laundering activities. Since it is estimated that $300 billion to $500 billion is cycled through the U.S. financial system on an annual basis, the operation will have little real effect. Federal officials expect to seize as much as $152 million in more than 100 accounts in the United States, Europe and the Caribbean. (Washington Post, May 20, 1998).

[72]"Clean Getaway for Money Launderers," Journal of Commerce, 10 December 1996, 62.

It does not take a criminal genius to figure out how to get around the US government reporting requirements and to launder money, and the big guys can afford to hire all the lawyers and others to take care of the problem for them. In addition, according to former Federal Reserve Board Governor Lawrence Lindsey, the money-laundering laws discriminate against the poor. They are the least likely to have established relationships with banks and the most likely to operate primarily with cash. Hence, they are the first to be targeted, and this even further discourages bankers from wanting their business.

Anyone willing to devote a little intelligence, time and effort to laundering money can now do so, and will be able to under almost any conceivable regulation, with only a minuscule chance of being convicted. The real total cost for each money laundering conviction per year appears to be over a hundred million dollars. The costs to the banks run in the tens of billions of dollars; the costs of the Federal government enforcement efforts run into the low billions of dollars. These costs result in higher bank charges, higher taxes, and lower quality financial services for Americans. If the money laundering war were a shooting war, and if it cost a hundred million or even a million dollars for each enemy fatality, America would have been bankrupted after its first major battle. Or to look at it in another way, if the real total cost of the war on money laundering is only $10 billion, it is roughly equal to what the Federal government spends on child nutrition programs. Other law enforcement endeavors surely could spend money to better effect.

Members of Congress and others have attacked Judge Starr and other "Special Prosecutors" for the cost of each conviction, yet their average cost per conviction is a fraction of the average real cost per conviction of each money launderer.

The government financial regulators will claim that, even though they cannot justify the costs they impose on an expense-conviction basis, their activities have a major deterrent effect. They will provide data to show that when they target a particular geographical area, the number of currency wire transfers declines. In reality, people merely move their activity to a different location once the targeting orders are announced. It is equivalent to squeezing a balloon.

By any fair, objective standard, the war on money laundering has been a colossal failure. It has not hurt drug dealers, terrorists, or assorted criminals. It has hurt the American taxpayer and financial institutions. It has only benefited those in government who owe their jobs to the enforcement effort. The war on money laundering has in reality been a war on the pocketbooks and civil liberties of the American people, carried out by government bureaucrats.

Excuses for Destroying Financial Privacy

The business of everybody is the business of nobody.

−Lord MacCauley

Countries like Switzerland have maintained financial privacy for their citizens, have lower crime rates than the US, and Swiss citizens are no more subject to terrorism than Americans. The following table compares the number of crimes recorded by the police, broken into crime categories (all figures are quoted per 100,000 people):[73]

---

[73]Homicide is defined as the intentional killing of a person; violent crimes include violence against the person, robbery and sexual offenses; drug trafficking offenses include illegal importing, exporting or supplying of narcotic drugs; domestic burglary is defined as gaining access to a dwelling by the use of force to steal goods. The information recorded in the above table was extrapolated from the report, "Criminal Statistics: England and Wales 1996, Statistics relating to Crime and Criminal Proceedings for the year 1996," which was available from the Bureau of Justice Statistics in Washington, DC.

Country	Homicides	Violent Crimes	Drug Trafficking	Burglaries
Switzerland	2.8	97.5	35.4	1045.7
United States	7.4	633.7	567 (estimated)	942.3

Of course, there are cultural reasons beyond law that help explain the difference in crime levels of the US and Switzerland or several other countries. Nevertheless, the Swiss have proved that you can have low crime and financial privacy. The Swiss borders are no less porous than the US and they are no more restrictive on trade and capital flows.

The major policy reason given for the destruction of financial privacy is that it is the only way to combat the crime of money laundering. Officials of the Financial Crimes Enforcement Network (FinCEN) of the Treasury Department will also tell you that most attempts at money laundering come about from the illegal drug trade. But the attempts to curtail drug use by chasing money launderers has been a particularly obvious and spectacular failure. The notion that a drug dealer is going to stop pushing drugs on kids because of the present minuscule chance that he might be convicted of money laundering lacks any grounding in reality. The rewards for pushing drugs are considered to be worth much greater risks.

As previously noted, the few people that the government has been able to convict of money laundering have been mostly small dealers who did not have the sophistication to get around the existing restrictions. The real "drug king pins" have the money to buy the talent to get them around the anti-money laundering cops, and that is why the whole effort against money laundering has been so costly and ineffective.

Advocates of anti-money-laundering legislation argue that it is important in combating organized crime. Unfortunately, there is as much evidence that anti-money laundering activities by the government, like Prohibition in the 1920s, are more apt to create organized crime than to curtail it. Such activity creates a market for more sophisticated money handlers, thus increasing the size of the criminal network. Hence crime groups are strengthened by having the additional "product line" of money laundering services to offer the common criminal. To expand their money laundering business, the organized leaders have a vested interest in increasing the number of local drug pushers and common thieves. FinCEN recently claimed that the precious metals industry had been criminalized by money launderers. Assuming that this assertion by FinCEN is true, it is likely that the mere existence of the anti-money-laundering cops helped turn a non-criminal industry into a criminal one.

Anti-money-laundering advocates also argue that their efforts strengthen our national defense against terrorism and outlaw regimes. No one wants to help the terrorist, but again, where is the evidence that any significant terrorist group had been deterred by the anti-money laundering cops? There may be a few cases where some disgruntled individuals or small groups were detected by the anti-money laundering network, but there is no evidence that any major terrorist activity has been deterred. Despite the loss of our financial privacy, the World Trade Center and Oklahoma City bombings occurred, and in neither of these cases are there indications that they were undertaken by very sophisticated groups. A serious, sophisticated terrorist group would have little difficulty evading the anti-money laundering cops.

Terrorism is a real threat, and that is why it is so important not to waste money and police resources on measures that do not work. The money and effort should be spent on activities that are much more cost effective, and less intrusive.

The digital technology that has made it more difficult to tap phone lines and read encrypted messages has also made it easier for law enforcement to monitor the whereabouts of individuals (through video cameras and "electronic tags"), and to listen in passively on conversations at considerable distances. If anything, overall law enforcement agencies have an increased advantage against criminals because of the new technologies, thus the cries about losing the competitive advantage in encryption are greatly overstated.

Who Benefits from the Destruction of Financial Privacy

Giving money and power to government is like giving whiskey and car keys to teenage boys.

—PJ O'Rourke

Why, then, when it is so obvious that tens of billions of dollars are being wasted in the anti-money laundering fight, is it not abandoned? The answer is that there are strong vested interests in waging the war but not in winning the battles.

Politicians who do not have a clue about how to stop drug dealing and organized crime can claim they are doing "something"—because few ever look to see if the "something" is counterproductive. Politicians also gain power and influence by being able to control others. Destroying financial privacy gives both political leaders and bureaucrats knowledge of the affairs of others, and knowledge is power.

Those who are philosophical statists, or those in government who merely like having their domains enlarged, tend to be strong advocates of anti-money laundering activities. It provides another excuse to increase taxes and hire more regulators, thus increasing government's power.

Once the anti-money laundering bureaucracies are established (*i.e.*, FinCEN, plus the FBI, and Federal Reserve Board offices), the bureaucrats have a very strong vested interest in having them maintained and enlarged. It is human nature not to want to have your job abolished. Most people wish to have their empires enlarged even though their activities might be totally useless. When is the last time a group of government bureaucrats went to the public and the Congress to advocate the abolition of their agency? Most government bureaucrats are fine people, but the incentive structure leads good people to do stupid and sometimes bad things. Officials are often shameless, or worse, in their efforts to preserve their own agencies.

There are now literally tens of thousands of government workers who are involved in financial regulation, or whose jobs depend on having extensive financial regulation and reporting requirements. These government workers and their families and friends are a strong and politically sophisticated special interest group. They can be expected to fight to the bitter end to maintain their regulatory authority over activities which can no longer effectively be regulated. Given that they are trapped in technological obsolescence, many will act like any trapped animal and lash out in a wild and (verbally) violent manner to those who paint the picture of reality—which will be their professional death.

Fortunately, most of these financial regulatory bureaucrats are intelligent, well-educated people who will be able to find other good jobs, most of which will be far less destructive to economic growth and individual liberty.

Chapter V

OPPRESSION, PRIVACY AND FREEDOM

Despots themselves do not deny that freedom is excellent only they desire it for themselves alone, and they maintain that everyone else is altogether unworthy of it.

—Alexis de Tocqueville

The Totalitarians

The modern assault on financial freedom and privacy began in earnest with the Bolshevik revolution in Russia in 1917. The Red Terror that Lenin unleashed in order to nationalize industry and collectivize agriculture had ruined industry by 1920 and caused mass starvation by 1921. Russia was rapidly industrializing before World War I. Production had increased by 62% from 1900 to 1913 and continued to increase up through 1916, despite Russia's involvement in World War I. Yet in 1920, after only three years of communist rule, total output of manufactured goods had fallen to a mere 12.9% of the prewar level.[74]

The communists denied the rights of private property and financial privacy, on the basis of Karl Marx's thesis that an individual could only be "a public person." The collective was supreme over the individual, and hence there was no right to an individual personal life, let alone a right to privacy.

Bulgaria, which was taken over by the communists in 1947, is a typical example of what happens to individual liberties and financial privacy under a communist regime. The communists put in their own Constitution, which stated: "The forms of property in the People's Republic of Bulgaria are: state (public), cooperative, public organizations' property, and personal property" (Chapter II, Article 14). Personal property referred to such small items as a person's toothbrush. All land and enterprises, including banks, were owned by the state. The communist party was considered supreme and by definition beneficent, hence there was no need for financial privacy. Those who resisted, or asserted that their individual or economic rights ought to be recognized, were put in concentration camps or killed. In Bulgaria, approximately 180,000 people, out of a population of eight and half million, were imprisoned.

All economic activity was regulated in very precise detail under the Bulgarian communist regime and presented in the State Gazette.[75] People could incur severe penalties for even the most insignificant infringements. For instance, business trips abroad were regulated in an exacting manner. (One item in these regulations gave a precise table for daily allowances and hotel expenses for different countries; another set a 15-day term for submitting a detailed financial report, and a

---

[74]Paul Johnson, Modern Times: The World from the Twenties to the Eighties (New York: Harper & Row Publishers, Inc., 1983), 88.
[75]State Gazette No. 74, (September 18, 1973), 2.

30-day term for returning currency which had not been spent). Prosecutors were allowed to see the details of a person's bank account in the State Savings Bank (DSK) without a court order. One regulation (Article 15-2) required that currency taken abroad without permission of the Ministry of Finance be confiscated by the customs officer. In the same set of financial regulations, Article 50 stated that when one purchased foreign currency for the payment of fees, visas, tickets for foreign countries, insurance, purchases of goods and services and other special purposes, one must describe in detail the purpose of purchasing the foreign currency. These and other regulations were put into effect by a totalitarian regime in Bulgaria to deny all financial privacy. What is frightening is how closely they resemble (if only in an extreme form) some of the recent US Treasury Department regulations concerning the right to seize currency and to peer into bank accounts, using the threats of drugs and terrorism as the excuses.

Full-fledged currency controls and so-called "inconvertibility of currencies" are a twentieth century invention, first developed by Hitler's economic minister, Hjalmar Schacht, in the 1930s. Before Hitler, there were many occasions when countries were unwilling or unable to convert their paper currency into gold or silver, and that was referred to as inconvertibility. However, as Milton Friedman notes, that did not mean "that a country prohibited its citizens or residents from trading pieces of paper promising to pay specified sums in the monetary unit to that country for corresponding pieces of paper expressed in the monetary unit of another country—or for that matter coin or bullion."[76] The German Nazis were the first to do that.

Hitler effectively extinguished all personal freedom in Germany, including all financial freedom, with his Emergency Decree of February 28, 1933, "For the Protection of the

[76]Milton Friedman, Capitalism and Freedom (Chicago: University of Chicago Press: 1962), 57-58.

People and the State."[77]   Along with other results, this decree
served to confiscate "anti-German" and Jewish wealth.   The
currency controls were designed to stop capital flight (*i.e.*, the
right of the people to try to protect their savings from seizure
by the state).   Many Germans, particularly German Jews, had been
sending their money to countries they viewed as safe havens, such as
Switzerland, the United Kingdom, and the United States.

After this declaration, it was clear that for the Jews and
others who opposed the Nazis, to remain in Germany was to
put oneself at great risk.   The Nazis began arresting German
citizens in 1933, forcing them to sign papers giving powers of
attorney to German officials to allow the officials to obtain
information from Swiss banks and insurance companies about
possible German bank deposits or insurance policies.   From
then on, many Germans and particularly German Jews were
very careful to avoid opening accounts in their own names,
and thus were forced to seek caretakers.   This practice helped
make it difficult for the Swiss banks and others to identify the
rightful owners of such accounts in the post-war years.

Hitler "regarded himself as a socialist, and the essence of
his socialism was that every individual or group in the state
should unhesitatingly work for national policy."[78]   The National Socialist regime did not require most property to be
owned by the state, as long as it was effectively controlled by
the state.   Thus the German people continued to own property, and
most industry remained in private hands, but the state actively regulated what could be done with the property and how it was managed.

Hitler and his cronies were not interested in constitutions
or the rule of law.   The government was largely operated by
decree and by the whims of those in control and, as a result,

[77]Paul Johnson, Modern Times: The World from the Twenties to the Eighties (New York:
Harper & Row Publishers, Inc., 1983), 285.
    [78]Ibid., 294.

there was no legally protected financial privacy. Hitler had learned from the mistakes of the communists and thus understood, as do modern-day regulators of private property, that it is possible to achieve the aims of restricting the liberty of property owners without owning the property outright.

Despite the collapse of communism and the defeat of national socialism and fascism, the ideological descendants of Lenin, Hitler, and Stalin are still with us. As one example, the country of Belarus has been suffering under a latter-day national socialist by the name of Alexander Lukashenko.[79] As Daniel Williams of the Washington Post reported:

> "For now, it is soft-core Stalinism," said Yuri Hashevatsky, who made a satirical documentary about Lukashenko that has never been shown. "You feel the tension grow. People have their houses searched. Tax inspectors harass opposition businesses. Police beat demonstrators."[80]

Democracy and Liberty

Democracy never lasts long. It soon wastes, exhausts, and murders itself. There has never been a democracy that did not commit suicide.

–John Adams

Americans used to think that intrusions into financial privacy and seizure of property without due process could only take place in totalitarian dictatorships. Now, unfortunately,

---

[79]In November 1996, I witnessed Lukashenko's police thugs drag the head of the election commission out of his office, in Minsk, Belarus, and dump him on the street shortly after I had met with him. The Commissioner owed his treatment to the fact that he had the audacity to publicly state that Lukashenko was rigging a referendum, which indeed was true. From interviews I conducted with members of the Belarus Supreme Soviet (their parliamentary body), I received first-hand testimony from those who had been put in jail with no formal charges filed against them.

[80]Daniel Williams, "Leaders are Marching Belarus Stalwartly into Soviet Era Past," Washington Post, 12 November 1997, A20.

increasing numbers know better. In attempts to gain political
popularity or power, the US Congress, the bureaucracy, and
the courts have all whittled away at the liberty of the
people under the guise of correcting real or imaginary
problems.

In 1933, at the time that the Nazis were instituting the
world's first modern currency controls, the Roosevelt Administration made it illegal for American citizens to hold or to buy
and sell gold (there were limited exemptions for the purchase
and manufacture of jewelry). Up to 1933, gold clause contracts had been popular for many types of obligations, such as
railroad bonds. As a result, after 1933, holders of such bonds
no longer could obtain settlement in gold. In essence, the US
government diminished the value of the bond holders' property without just compensation, an apparent violation of the
intent of the founding fathers in writing the Constitution.
Nevertheless, the gold restrictions were upheld by the courts,
and it was not until 1973 that American citizens regained the
right to buy and sell gold as they pleased.

America is still blessed with a number of brave reporters
and publishers who are beginning to shine the spotlight
of publicity on some of the more outrageous abuses. For
example, in a Forbes article, reporters Brigid McMenamin and Janet Novack wrote that more than 10,000 actions have been made into crimes by regulation. They
cite "Title 18, Section 1341 of the US Code says that any
act of dishonesty in which a mailed item (or, since 1952,
with the addition of Section 1343, a telephone call) plays
a role constitutes a federal crime."[81]   Tens of millions of
Americans might well be guilty of violations of this rule.
Further:

---

[81]Brigid McMenamin and Janet Novack, "The White-Collar Gestapo," Forbes. 1 December
1997, 88.

Under Title 7 of the US Code, Section 953, any "warehouseman, broker, cleaner, sheller, dealer, growers' cooperative association, salter, crusher or manufacturer of peanut products" who refuses to file reports "on the quantity of peanuts and peanut oil received, processed, shipped and owned by him" can be hit with a year in jail.[82]

No longer are the legislators alone legislating. This trend allowing regulations to have the force of law in effect invites unelected bureaucrats to legislate.

McMenamin and Novack found countless examples of abuse of power and convictions on all manner of vague violations. For example, they report, "Michael Milken did time for activities such as 'aiding and abetting a net capital violation.' What is that exactly? Hard to say, but punishing Milken was a way to get even for the layoffs and plant closings and takeovers that took place in the 1980s."[83] McMenamin and Novack also found examples of sentences that were well over the maximum sentence guidelines, which were justified by the courts on the basis of charges of which the accused had not been found guilty:

A White Plains, N.Y. federal jury in October 1996 convicted real estate lawyer Donal Walsh of making false statements on his application for a $330,000 home mortgage. At Walsh's sentencing, the judge doubled what would have been a maximum six-month sentence to a full year— in part because of six other conspiracy and

---

[82]Brigid McMenamin and Janet Novack, "The White-Collar Gestapo," <u>Forbes</u>. 1 December 1997, 94.
[83]Ibid., 86.

fraud charges on which Walsh had won acquittal.[84]

Another relatively new game in the prosecuting trap is the application of money-laundering charges to accompany a variety of petty financial crimes. For instance:

> To cover a cash flow problem in his casino, real estate and marina businesses, Florida businessman, James W. Maulden engineered a check-kiting scheme that involved 29 accounts at the Bay Bank & Trust Co. of Panama City, Fla., where he served as a director. Maulden always eventually covered the checks. Nevertheless, he was found guilty of bank fraud and misapplication of funds—punishable, his lawyer figures, by up to 16 months in jail in his case. But the Feds also convinced the court to convict him of money-laundering because he used some of the bad checks to pay off a loan from another bank. Result: ten years.[85]

Do not be sucked into the belief that you are immune to becoming the victim of such overreaching prosecution. McMenamin and Novack cite the following scenarios, which are among the thousands of possible minor actions that could cost you a great deal of time and expense, and possibly land you in jail:

> "You just mailed in a $1,200 expense account. One of the items was a $7 cab ride. That's what you said. Actually, you spent $5. You just committed a felony."

---

[84]Brigid McMenamin and Janet Novack, "The White-Collar Gestapo," Forbes. 1 December 1997, 94.
[85]Ibid., 96.

"You're on the beach in Hawaii and you send a postcard to your mother-in-law. 'Having a wonderful time,' you write. 'Wish you were here.' Felony? Who knows? Don't make any enemies in the Justice Department."[86]

As McMenamin and Novack explained, "A country can lose its liberties overnight in a coup d'état. It can also lose them bit by bit to a grasping bureaucracy, aided and abetted by a legislature prone to solving each new problem—real or perceived—with a criminal statute."[87] That is the great danger of criminalizing every manner of behavior that is viewed by some as unsavory or unbecoming.

As the number of criminal laws and regulations has expanded, so has the temptation to use them for political advantage. Clearly, a democracy cannot be sustained if the party in power seeks to silence its opponents and critics though police actions by the state. There have been abuses all through American history, including the Watergate scandal of the Nixon Administration. However, the Clinton Administration seems to be reaching a new and unprecedented level of abuse. As the columnist and senior fellow at the Cato Institute, Doug Bandow, has noted:

> The Administration has politicized the FBI, using it to justify the White House Travel Office purge. Presidential aides snooped through FBI files on potential Administration opponents. The IRS is auditing not only Paula Jones, who has accused Bill Clinton of sexual harassment, but a suspiciously large number of conservative foundations and groups. No liberal organizations are undergoing similar reviews. The

White House pressured the Treasury Department over the latter's probe of Madison Guar-
anty, which financed the Clinton's Whitewater
investment.[88]

The Administration also seems to believe that the FBI and
Justice Departments need to be granted even more powers
with which to round up information on citizens. Bandow
notes these expansions:

> The Administration, the most wiretap-
> friendly in US history, has sought to eliminate
> Fourth Amendment protections against govern-
> ment searches. The President claims to possess
> "inherent authority to conduct warrantless
> searches for foreign intelligence purposes." ...
> President Clinton pushed the Communications
> Assistance [for Law Enforcement] Act, which
> requires telephone companies to retrofit their
> systems to ease police surveillance, supported
> restrictions on the sale of Internet encryption
> technology, and requested legislation forcing
> firms to give the government "keys" to such
> technology.[89]

At the same time, the Administration and the Congress are
trying to put greater restrictions on, and criminalize more of,
the behavior of average Americans. The papers are filled with
almost daily revelations about wrongdoing and criminal behavior at the highest levels of government. The Treasury Department and the Justice Department, including the FBI, have the
responsibility for enforcing most of the laws pertaining to
money laundering and other financial crimes. But what have

---

[88]Doug Bandow, "Clinton's Brand of Jackboot Liberalism," Washington Times 19 October
1997, B3.
[89]Ibid.

these officials been doing? A few examples from the newspapers in the late fall of 1997 are indicative of the situation.

On November 3, 1997, the Washington Times reported that a senior official in the US Department of the Treasury, Office of the Inspector General, "admitted destroying a critical document that showed that two Secret Service agents are under investigation for possible perjury for their testimony last year about the FBI Filegate affair." A week later, on November 11, the Washington Times reported that, after reviewing a GAO report on the corruption in the Treasury Inspector General's Office, Senator Susan Collins (ME) wrote, "The review uncovered clear, credible and disturbing evidence that the inspector general misused her position by steering a $90,000 sole-source contract for a management study to her longtime acquaintance, a person who wrote a letter of recommendation on her behalf [to the White House] for the position of inspector general."[90] Senator Richard Shelby (AL) further noted that the GAO found that there had been "a concerted effort to hide the truth about an investigation that should have never been opened in the first place."[91] The Inspector General is supposed to prevent crime in the Treasury Department, not to initiate and participate in it. If the cop's cop engages in illegal behavior, how much can you trust the government to protect rather than harm the citizens?

The following month, on December 9, 1997, the Financial Times did a review of what had been happening at the nation's top law enforcement agency, the FBI, for the last three years. They noted that since FBI director Louis Freeh took charge of the agency, the following incidents had occurred:

---

[90]Ruth Larson, "Senators Pressure Treasury to Fire Inspector General," Washington Times, 11 November 1997, A6.
[91]Ibid.

- the disaster of the Branch Davidian siege in Waco, Texas;
- a blistering report on the quality of forensic evidence from the FBI's crime laboratory;
- the slandering of the hapless Richard Jewell, the security guard who spotted the Atlanta Olympic bomb;
- the Bureau's destruction of an internal critique of its mishandling of the Ruby Ridge siege in 1992 when agents shot dead a mother and her daughter;
- the revelation that one of its agents spied for Moscow.[92]

These types of activities by US government officials are both sad and frightening. The fact is, the American people are too often at risk to be abused rather than protected by those with the police powers in Washington. The abuses again illustrate how right Lord Acton was about the corruption of power. That is why it is so important that the people be allowed to have the tools they need—such as unfettered access to high grade public-key encryption—to protect themselves against corrupt and incompetent government officials.

Financial Crimes and the Telecommunications Industry

In the US and many other countries, the telephone companies have been forced to help government law enforcement agencies for many years. When the FBI or some other law enforcement agency obtains a court order for a telephone "wiretap," it requires the telephone company to set up the tap. With the old analog telephone communications system, this was an easy process from a technical standpoint. However, in

[92]Nicholas Timmins, "Bungles, Mishaps, and Tension Dog FBI," Financial Times 9 December 1997, 7.

the digital age, and particularly with digital encryption, the process becomes far more complex. As already noted, large-bit encryption is almost impossible to break. Thus the US government has argued for regulations limiting the size of encryption (to 40 bits at the time of this writing), and access to a "key" to read the encrypted material.

The FBI has been lobbying for digital telephony plans for most of the decade. Their digital telephony plans require every communications system in the country to install software to facilitate wiretaps. In late 1994, "digital telephony" was passed by the Congress and signed into law by President Clinton. This measure will cost the telephone companies and ultimately their customers billions of dollars, and serve almost no useful purpose.

The Clinton Administration had been trying to require the use of the "Clipper chip," which is an NSA-designed chip, created for encrypting voice communications. The Clipper chip includes a "key escrow" system that could be used by authorized government agencies to decode messages encoded by the device. For obvious reasons, there has been much resistance to the adoption of the Clipper chip. The Clipper chip is now "voluntary," meaning that it will only be used by those who do not mind the government monitoring their communications.

Telecommunications companies see the Internet as a big growth area of their business. They understand that many of their customers will be reluctant to use the Internet if they cannot have secure encryption, and 40-bit encryption is no longer secure. Secondly, customers are unlikely to feel comfortable with government agents having access to the key. The government has proposed that all the "keys" be put in an escrow depository. The idea is foolhardy. If a wrongdoer wanted to create true chaos, what better place to break into than the "key depository?"

Who would you trust to guard the depository?   Webb
Hubbell?   Or, perhaps you would choose Gerald P. Murray, a
deputy chief financial officer with the US Department of
Treasury's Financial Crimes Enforcement Network.   Mr. Murray, who surely is usually a nice man, was convicted of assault
and destruction of property July 10, 1997, after he slammed
on his brakes in front of the car of a young woman, forcing her
to stop her car on the Washington Beltway.   Murray then got
out of his car and walked up to the young woman's window,
yelling for her to open her window.   When she did not, he
smashed the glass and reached in to grab her throat.   Mr.
Murray later expressed his "sincere apology," explaining that
the incident was totally out of character. [93]   Nonetheless, his
story does exemplify the truth that even government officials
can become nasty and act out of character, and it is possible
that they can even do a great deal of damage.   Imagine how
much more damage could be done when they are given access
to very personal and sensitive information unnecessarily.

Some government officials have demanded that the phone
companies have the power to decrypt anything that comes
over their wires in an encrypted format, and then be willing to
turn it over to the government.   The fact that such proposals
could even be seriously considered shows how fragile our
remaining liberty is.

The telephone companies have not been as effective as
they should have in protecting their shareholders and customers from the outrageous demands made of them by the
FBI and other agencies.   Their impotence in part comes from
the fact that they hire lawyers and others who are not committed to free market democratic capitalism and the common
good, and hence make weak-kneed and unprincipled arguments before the Congress and regulatory agencies.

[93]Wendy Melillo, "Va. Motorist Gets One Year for Attacking Woman" Washington Post 19
September 1997.

The phone companies are faced with potential costs reaching hundreds of millions—if not billions—of dollars to provide information that flows across their lines to government agencies. Of course, quaint concepts of cost-benefit analyses or the loss of freedom are beneath the bureaucrats who dream up such schemes. The folks in government tell the phone companies to pass along the costs to the customers. The result is that everyone pays more for their phone service in order to reduce their own privacy.

Yet while all of these proposals place a huge financial and privacy cost on law-abiding citizens, they have virtually no effect on the bad guys because they are so easy to evade.

Internet or IP telephony—the technology that enables voice calls to be routed over data networks—is now a reality. Within a couple of years, consumers will be able to send long distance telephone calls through Internet phone lines, through the Internet over cable company lines, directly from hand-held phones to satellites, or through traditional phone lines. Given these multiple modes for sending encrypted messages, it is hard to see how interception by law-enforcement agencies could ever be cost-effective, given there will be tens of billions of call minutes.

Financial Freedom and the IRS

In the summer of 1997, as a result of the Senate Hearings on IRS abuses and the work of some good investigative reporters, Americans had their worst fears about the Internal Revenue Service confirmed. A sample of the findings conclude that the IRS:

♦ Especially abuses taxpayers whom agents feel
   are in a poor position to fight back;

- Explicitly engaged in practices designed to threaten and intimidate innocent taxpayers;
- Has an appallingly high error rate, and consistently bills taxpayers for money they do not owe;
- Has a quota system for collections, and many of the tax collectors do not care if the taxpayer did not owe what they demanded (which is explicitly illegal under the Taxpayer Bill of Rights, which the Congress passed in 1988);
- Has driven taxpayers to suicide;
- Refuses to pay judgments to taxpayers when it loses in court, and keeps litigating at taxpayer expense until the taxpayer is driven into bankruptcy or dies;
- Rarely disciplines or fires employees, even when they violate the law.

Further,

- Employees violated the right to confidentiality by looking at returns of friends, relatives, and enemies;
- Record-keeping is in shambles, and taxpayer records have been deliberately destroyed;
- Accounting practices are so bad that audits of the books have not been able to be made for four years.

These are not mere allegations; the agency ultimately acknowledged their truth. Months before the hearings, Ann Reilly Dowd of Money Magazine got it exactly right when she wrote:

Dear Internal Revenue Service:

Our two-month audit of your operations has determined that you are guilty of sloppy, discourteous and sometimes devious behavior. Your practices are so unacceptable, in fact, that if you were a US taxpayer, your pay could be garnished or your property seized. But you're no small-fry US taxpayer; you're the all-powerful IRS. So when you mess up, you draw little more than anguished cries from law-abiding citizens and lawmakers alike. Meanwhile, taxpayers are being punished by your agency's unrepentant abuse of decent, hard-working individuals.[94]

The irony is that the IRS does not have to act this way, nor did it in the past. Up until the last three decades, the tax system was largely a non-intrusive honor system. Your bank was not a spy for the IRS, and did not report your cash withdrawals or interest income. The only reports the IRS received about you were your wage withholding statements (a practice begun in the early 1940s). Stock and real estate transactions, dividends, and other income were not reported to the IRS. Individuals reported these sources of income at the end of the year. It was an honor system, compatible with a free society and, for the most part, it worked. It was an age when taxpayers were still considered innocent until proven guilty, in contrast to the present system in which the government does not have to prove guilt, but can wait for the accused to prove their innocence. (Part, but not all, of the "burden of proof" was shifted to the IRS by the Congress in 1998).

Part of the movement away from the honor system was a

---

[94]Anne Reilly Dowd, "Money Audits the IRS. If the IRS Were a Taxpayer, It Would Owe Big Fines for Misconduct. Instead, We All Foot the Bill for More than $5 Billion," Money Magazine (January 1997 Vol. 26 No. 1 n. pag.).

result of the new technologies (computers) that enabled government to keep detailed records of people's behavior, which before had not been possible. Of course, the point of this book is that the tide has turned, and now these same technologies are advancing to the time when individuals will be able to regain a good deal of the financial privacy they once enjoyed.

Not only has the IRS become far more intrusive, but the government has also become far more vindictive to citizens caught in its snares. In most countries, the sanction for a tax violation is a reasonable fine. Imprisonment for tax violations is rare and, when imposed, the sentences are usually short.

In the US, the situation is far less benign. A barbaric punishment was given to a lady in Kansas City in 1988, named Trula Walker. She was convicted for tax evasion and sentenced to thirty years in jail. (By contrast, people convicted on murder counts in Washington, DC are often out of jail within a couple of years). Leona Helmsley got four years in the penitentiary for her alleged tax offense, yet Sophia Loren was only restricted to a friend's home for thirty days for her offense of the same scale.[95]

America is supposed to be the home of the free, yet it shares with Sweden and the Soviet Union the global record for the most onerous and brutal penalties for tax evasion. However, modern non-communist Russia has only monetary penalties for tax evasion in all but the most extreme cases. Ironically, in the US "our tax bureaucracy is, indeed, like a miniature Soviet state with the power to intimidate just about everyone, and this is because of the synthetic crimes Congress has manufactured to make these tax police, especially the IRS criminal division, masters of the art of intimidation."[96]

[95]Charles Adams, For Good and Evil: The Impact of Taxes on the Course of Civilization (New York: Madison Books, 1993), 386.
[96]Ibid., 385.

The IRS has adopted a number of the old habits of totalitarian regimes, one of which is paying informers. If you give the IRS information that leads to a tax recovery, you can get as much as ten percent of the first $75,000, five percent of the next $25,000, and one percent of the additional amount recovered. Such behavior may be cost-effective for the IRS, but it engenders mistrust and deceit, rather than a civil society, which should be the object of good governance.

The good news is that the horror, corruption and abuse that people have been suffering at the hands of both totalitarian and democratic governments is not a necessary condition, nor one that should be as prevalent in the future. Let us now return to the country that perhaps has moved furthest toward having the set of policies and practices that is likely to be compatible with a prosperous and free society in the future: Switzerland.

The Future and the Swiss Model

A former French Finance Minister (who shall remain nameless) once said, "Switzerland is the mirror of our mistakes." Most people in the world can only dream about achieving what the Swiss have accomplished. They have ruled themselves by democratic means for hundreds of years, have an exceptionally high standard of living, low unemployment, almost no inflation, and low crime, and have been at peace with their neighbors for almost two centuries. In World War II, they remained the only democratic, capitalist country in continental Europe, even though they were entirely surrounded by the National Socialists.

At first glance, Switzerland seems an unlikely place for such success. It is small (about twice the size of Massachusetts) and mountainous, with a population of approximately seven

million people. It is surrounded by much larger nations who
have been frequently at war, and expansionary in their intent
for centuries. The Swiss speak several different languages,
including German, French, Italian, and Romansch, rather than
having a unifying national language.

The Switzerland that we know today began with the unifica-
tion of three cantons (local area governments) around Lake
Lucerne in 1291. Cantons were added and many conflicts
ensued, but by 1648, Switzerland was recognized by the
"Peace of Westphalia" as a completely independent state.
Except for the brief period when it was controlled by
Napoleonic France, Switzerland has managed to maintain its
independence. The Congress of Vienna in 1815 recognized
the perpetual neutrality of Switzerland, and the country's
borders have remained fixed from that time.

After many early squabbles, the Swiss learned that they
were all better off tolerating the differences among themselves,
while at the same time having a strong unified national defense. Their toleration of language and religious differences
caused them to establish strong local governments at the
canton (county) and commune (town) levels, and a small
national government. Government activity, as well as most
government spending and taxing, is concentrated at the local
level. Most people do not know or remember the name of
their current President, because his or her power is so limited
that it is not important. Some of the cantons and communes
have small and low-tax governments, while others have fairly
large semi-socialistic governments. Taxes at the national or
"Confederation" level are low, but total tax burdens can be
quite high in some of the communes and cantons. However,
on average, the Swiss have a far lower tax burden than the
citizens of most industrialized countries.

The Swiss have succeeded in part because they have

remembered what we Americans and others have forgotten—that liberty requires privacy, particularly financial privacy. As M. Bonvin, of the Swiss Federal Council, stated in 1967, "In the view of the Swiss people, the freedom of the individual takes precedence over the fiscal interests (of the state), even on the risk that this freedom is sometimes misused."[97] Switzerland is much more of a direct democracy than is the US or most other Western nations. The Swiss require that proposals to increase the salary of legislators or to increase taxes must be submitted to the voters for approval.

The Swiss continue to understand that they will no longer be free if they tolerate prying by their own government, let alone foreign governments. This view has brought them into conflict with US and other foreign authorities who want to investigate Swiss bank records.[98] Swiss bank privacy was maintained for centuries as a matter of custom and tradition.

Banking privacy in Switzerland is not absolute. It can be waived in cases in which it is proved that a criminal act (as defined under Swiss law) has occurred and involves funds that have been deposited in a Swiss banking institution. The Swiss assert that there are some acts which are considered crimes in other jurisdictions, that are not, in the Swiss view, real crimes. These are most often "revenue crimes," such as tax avoidance, and violations of currency and exchange controls. For the most part, such acts are criminalized by governments which have engaged in financial malfeasance and have thereby created conditions that harm their citizens and make it difficult

---

[97] Charles Adams, For Good and Evil: The Impact of Taxes on the Course of Civilization (New York: Madison Books, 1993), 177.

[98] The Swiss have no interest in encouraging tax evasion, and do give some limited administrative assistance to foreign countries: Switzerland grants only very limited administrative assistance based on agreements concluded with third countries. The purpose of these agreements is to avoid double-taxation rather than to make it possible to apply the domestic law of the other contracting party. Generally speaking, the agreements concluded between Switzerland and other States are applied only at the request of the taxpayer. Yet Switzerland believes that tax evasion should be discouraged. For this reason, Switzerland laid down the 35% withholding tax on dividends and interest.

for citizens to protect their savings. The Swiss recognize that individuals have the inherent right to protect themselves against governments that make their currency worthless through inflation and impose currency controls, and from punitive tax regimes that are used to inflict pain on political enemies or use tax revenues for the direct benefit of those in power or their cronies.

Switzerland has become a major world financial center because over the centuries it has developed the reputation, among such clients as governments, corporations, and individuals, for political stability, responsibility, quality of service, privacy and financial freedom. In addition, the country has an outstanding transportation and telecommunications infrastructure. Many Swiss banks have a tradition going back centuries for international service and unparalleled financial integrity. The larger ones are universal banks, which provide full banking services, and have offices in many countries.

The Swiss concept of financial privacy is consistent with traditional English common law, where a man's home was his castle. Each castle had a private treasury, which was to be protected from the king's snooping. The English had learned that once the king knew what was in the treasury, he would often figure out a way to steal it. What the English and the Americans failed to realize, and the Swiss have done, is that the modern version of the castle treasury is the commercial bank account, and thus it should be beyond the surveillance of the king (or government).[99]

Those who signed the Magna Carta in that field at Runnymede, England in 1215 understood that financial privacy is necessary for individual liberty. Our American founding fathers also understood that concept.

---

[99]Charles Adams, For Good and Evil: The Impact of Taxes on the Course of Civilization (New York: Madison Books, 1993), 184.

In the digital age, successful governments will allow their own citizens and others financial privacy, because they will realize that technology makes it inevitable and that liberty demands it. The Swiss are furthest along this route to freedom and prosperity, and thus are most likely to be one of the earliest beneficiaries of digital liberation. Fortunately, others are learning these lessons, and are likely to be strong competitors to the Swiss, particularly if the Swiss continue to give ground to the demands of countries like the US. Also, the Swiss have been slow to embrace the Internet and 24-hour banking, and hence are in danger of seeing their market share drop if they do not move quickly to the digital age.

Chapter VI

WHY THE DIGITAL AGE
REQUIRES FREE TRADE
AND BANKING AND
FINANCIAL FREEDOM

No nation was ever ruined by trade.

—Benjamin Franklin

International Trade and the Digital Age

By the year 2002, Internet commerce is forecast to exceed $300 billion.[100] This trade will undermine many existing businesses, and present enormous opportunities to new businesses, because many of the traditional constraints of location, scale and time zones will disappear. Cyberstores may be located anywhere, and thus natural boundaries for many goods and services will become increasingly irrelevant.

For more than two hundred years, every good economist

---

[100]US Department of Commerce estimate as reported in the Financial Times by Vanessa Houlder, "Fear and enterprise on the net," May 20, 1998, p. 22.

has known that free trade is superior to protectionism in securing the well-being of the people. The fact that few countries have totally free trade is both a tragedy and a reflection of how little influence economists have on economic policy which, in the end, is decided by politicians.

In the age of digital money it will be increasingly difficult for governments to enact and enforce tariff and trade barriers, particularly on services—and this is all for the good.

It is no coincidence that the freest and most successful economies in the world also happen to have minimal trade barriers, while most of the relatively poor and unsuccessful countries have very high trade barriers. According to the 1998 Index of Economic Freedom, published by the Heritage Foundation and the Wall Street Journal, the five freest political entities and their average tariff rates are:

Country	Average Tariff Rate (%)
Hong Kong	0.0
Singapore	0.4
New Zealand	3.2
Switzerland	1.7
United States	3.3

This group of five are also characterized by having very high per capita incomes and close to full employment. Contrast this with some of the major countries that have low incomes and a high percentage of their populations living in poverty:

Country	Average Tariff Rate (%)
India	47.8
Bulgaria	18.0
China	23.0
Russia	10.7
Nigeria	18.3

A tariff reduces the real incomes of the people in the country levying the tariff, by requiring them to pay more for goods and services than other people in the world have to pay.

Those who advocate protectionism only show their ignorance of sound economic theory, not to mention the empirical results of endless experimentation of almost every possible type of trade policy by countries located on every continent. The results of these endless experiments are unambiguous—free trade is beneficial, and protectionism in all of its many forms is harmful.

The advantages of free trade were well recognized by the earliest of modern economists, including the great Finnish economist and clergyman Anders Chydenius who, in his book The National Gain, published in Swedish in 1765, gave the following example.

> Peasants [from several Finnish coastal villages] are almost indefatigable in making wooden articles. All through the winter the worker is hard at work making all kinds of wooden vessels as early as one or two o'clock in the morning, and thus he can sell his goods cheaper than anybody ... though many others along the coast have not only a better supply of forests, but also of workmen well versed in this trade. Let us look for the cause of this. It is quite impossible that such diligence could arise and be maintained without freedom of Export.
>
> ... The Staple Towns have often tried to deprive them of this privilege, but up till now been unsuccessful. ...
>
> But had the prohibition been successful, the

sales would of necessity have been limited, and consequently production to the same extent. Limited production makes idle hands and expensive goods, and if it should one day happen that other towns are allowed to stop these sales or prevent workmen from free occupation, then it is as certain as that two and two make four that Stockholm would have to buy more expensive wooden vessels than before, these towns would have their trade reduced, the country would lose inhabitants and earnings and the State its gain.[101]

Adam Smith's An Inquiry into the Nature and Causes of The Wealth of Nations, first published in Britain in 1776, is on almost everyone's list of the most important books ever written, and for very good reason. It is a book written by a man of vast learning and an extraordinary intellect, dealing with economics, philosophy, ethics, history, and political theory, as well as practical governance. Smith, who was a friend of Benjamin Franklin, had a profound influence on the American founding fathers, and on almost every learned individual who has been concerned with political economy in the intervening 220-plus years. Smith was almost certainly not aware of Chydenius' writings, given that they were in Swedish and published while Smith's work on Wealth of Nations was underway. (This was well before the age of instant translation and wide dissemination).

There is a twenty-page chapter in Wealth of Nations, Book IV, Chapter II, that should be required reading for anyone who aspires to hold political office. No one has better explained the advantages of trade and the folly of protectionism than Smith, and thus a couple of excerpts are worth repeating here:

---

[101] Anders Chydenius, The National Gain, trans. Georg Schauman (Great Britain, 1931), 74-75.

To give the monopoly of the home-market to the produce of domestic industry, in any particular art or manufacture, is in some measure to direct private people in what manner they ought to employ their capitals, and must, in almost all cases, be either a useless or a hurtful regulation. If the produce of domestic can be brought there as cheap as that of foreign industry, the regulation is evidently useless. If it cannot, it must generally be hurtful. It is the maxim of every prudent master of a family, never to attempt to make at home what it will cost him more to make than to buy. The taylor does not attempt to make his own shoes, but buys them of the shoemaker. The shoemaker does not attempt to make his own clothes, but employs a taylor. The farmer attempts to make neither the one nor the other, but employs different artificers. All of them find it for their interest to employ their whole industry in a way in which they have some advantage over their neighbours, and to purchase with a part of its produce, or what is the same thing, with the price of a part of it, whatever else they have occasion for.[102]

Smith further explains that what is true for an individual as to the advantage of trade, is also true for a country, regardless of the degree of advantage.

The natural advantages which one country has over another in producing particular commodities are sometimes so great, that it is acknowledged by all the world to be in vain to

---

[102]Adam Smith, <u>The Wealth of Nations</u>, (1776; New York: The Modern Library, 1937), 423-424.

struggle with them. By means of glasses, hotbeds, and hotwalls, very good grapes can be raised in Scotland, and very good wine too can be made of them at about thirty times the expence for which at least equally good can be brought from foreign countries. Would it be a reasonable law to prohibit the importation of all foreign wines, merely to encourage the making of claret and burgundy in Scotland? But if there would be a manifest absurdity in turning towards any employment, thirty times more of the capital and industry of the country, than would be necessary to purchase from foreign countries an equal quantity of the commodities wanted, there must be an absurdity, though not altogether so glaring, yet exactly of the same kind, in turning towards any such employment a thirtieth, or even a three hundredth part more of either. Whether the advantages which one country has over another, be natural or acquired, is in this respect of no consequence. As long as the one country has those advantages, and the other wants them, it will always be more advantageous for the latter, rather to buy of the former than to make.[103]

What Smith wrote was correct in 1776 and it is correct now.

Those who argue that free trade causes Americans to lose jobs and depresses wages ignore the fact that America has been creating jobs at a rapid rate, even in manufacturing, and that real wages have been rising, despite our movement towards lower tariffs and free trade agreements (like NAFTA).

---

[103]Adam Smith, The Wealth of Nations, (1776; New York: The Modern Library, 1937), 425-426.

As noted, real per capita incomes are highest in the US, Switzerland, and Hong Kong, entities which have minimal trade barriers. When someone buys an import for a lower price than they could make or buy a domestic alternative, he has more money left over to buy other things (or to invest). The additional spending resulting from the fact that consumers can obtain lower-priced imports results in higher domestic spending on other items and more investment, both of which serve to create more jobs and increase domestic productivity.

Protectionism has its great friends and supporters, and they are most often the ones being protected. That tariffs hurt the consumer is of little concern to most businessmen and union members in the protected business. Look closely at almost any protectionist and you will find that he represents a special interest. If union leaders were required to tell the truth, they would have to tell their members that the measures they are supporting actually would increase the prices they pay (thereby reducing the members' real incomes) in order to protect the jobs of a few other members for a period of time.

When some of the leaders of the Democratic Party in the US Congress say they care about consumers but oppose free trade legislation, such as giving the President "fast track authority" (a provision allowing the President to negotiate trade agreements that can only be voted up or down, without amendment, by the Senate), they can only be labeled as hypocrites or economic illiterates. These congressional "know nothings" will become the flat earthers of the digital age. Obviously, it is difficult to see all those new jobs that are created by free trade, since they are scattered across the economic landscape while, at the same time, it is easy to see those jobs that are lost because, most often, they are concentrated in a particular company or industry. Nevertheless, we have a right to expect our elected leaders to understand that subtleties in a situation occasionally reveal that the more readily perceived effects are not always the reality.

The volume of international trade around the globe has been growing far more rapidly than economic growth in general. This explosion in the growth of trade is a result of declining transportation costs and a reduction in trade barriers. Imports and exports in the US now equal about 20% of Gross Domestic Product (GDP), and 37% of the GDP of the European Union. For some of the smaller trading nations, trade accounts for well over half of their GDP.

The fastest growing segment of international trade is the trade in services. This type of trade consists of travel services, financial services (including insurance, legal and accounting services), sex talk and videos, architectural and engineering services, royalty and license fees, and miscellaneous business services. The US trade in services was over $400 billion in 1996, accounting for more than 5% of US GDP. Unlike trade in goods, the US has been running a surplus in services trade for more than two decades. The surplus in the service account was more than $80 billion in 1996.[104]

Much of the service trade can be conducted over the Internet or by other international electronic communication. To the extent it is done over the Internet, the "transportation cost" of the service begins to approach zero. As described in Chapter III, easy-to-use encryption—that not even the government can read without the expenditure of excessive resources—is becoming widely available. If both the service and the payment can be delivered over the Internet in encrypted form, it would be almost impossible for the government to collect a tax (tariff) on the transaction, in part because there would be no way of knowing that the transaction ever took place.

---

[104]US Department of Commerce, Bureau of Economic Analysis.

For instance, if someone decides to set up a foreign corporation in a tax-free jurisdiction, and he chooses to use a lawyer in a foreign country, the lawyer could do the necessary work, and send it by encrypted e-mail, without his own government knowing that he had done it. The lawyer could then direct that an encrypted payment be sent to an account controlled by the lawyer in another country.

A software firm decides to sub-contract some of its software product development to software writers in Russia. The product can be transferred over the Internet, and again an entity (not necessarily a bank) in some third country that does not levy an income tax could be designated as the recipient of the payment for the software.

Endless examples and variations can be created, but the point is that the digital world is going to make it very easy to hide the nature and origin of a product and payment that can be transmitted over the Internet. What the taxman cannot see, he cannot tax. What the regulator cannot detect, he cannot regulate. Given that it is now so easy, and will become much easier, to evade taxes on many international services, or even products like software, it is foolhardy for governments to attempt to put duties on such products.

Over time, most governments will learn the lesson and abolish duties on services and products that can be sold and delivered over the Internet. Unfortunately, some governments will lag in the process of reform, because of phony projected revenue loss estimates, or a desire to retain the ability to prosecute selectively. These laggard governments will experience capital flight, as well as a loss of business that can be conducted over the Internet by honest business people who would both prefer to obey the law and minimize taxes. In an age when some businesses can be moved electronically to another country in a matter of hours, unlike the years or months it took with traditional businesses, an unfriendly act by a government—such as a new tax or regulation—could cause businesses to flee in the same way that capital does. Honest business people will electronically move their businesses to friendly environments, which are most often characterized by low taxes and sensible regulation.

Commerce over the Internet is growing at an exponential rate. As early as the year 2000, Internet commerce is likely to be well over one trillion dollars.

Bank Regulation in the Digital Age

Our government has recently unleashed the greatest avalanche of regulations in peacetime history; and wherever we examine their working we see that they are using a sledgehammer to miss a nut.

—Christopher Booker[105]

Bank depositors naturally will seek to do business in markets with consumer-friendly regulation. Given the freedom to choose, they will shop for two principal qualities in selecting financial markets and institutions from among the available competitors:

1. protection of their deposits from loss;
2. protection of their financial privacy.

In almost all countries, a principal, stated intent of banking regulation is to provide reasonable protection to depositors from loss. While such regulations may be poorly designed, in

---

[105]English author and journalist. Qtd. in The Oxford Dictionary of Political Quotations, edited by Antony Jay.

some cases even counter-productive, at least there is no dis-agreement as to their ostensible objective. When it comes to privacy, by contrast, regulations in many (but fortunately not all) countries are anti-consumer, expressly intended to undermine privacy.

In the world of digital money, markets with regulatory regimes offering inadequate protection of deposits, privacy, or both, will lose deposits to competitors in pro-consumer environments. Furthermore, digital money will bring about changes in the nature of effective regulation, eventually making the regulator's task easier and further broadening the range of depositor choice. Until now, foreign exchange controls and geographic constraints have made possible the survival of banking regulations that do not protect depositors' money or their privacy. The digital age is rapidly removing these barriers.

Many less-developed countries have done a particularly poor job of maintaining the integrity of their banks and banking systems. Since 1980, there have been more than 100 banking crises in these countries. While some countries, such as Caribbean island tax havens, offer strong protection of banking privacy, depositors are wary of the stability of their banks, whether as a result of past incidents, political uncertainty, the inadequacy of information, or the inadequacy of regulatory regimes. Many other countries, such as the United States, do a good job of protecting deposits from loss while demonstrating a disregard for privacy. There are few countries, Switzerland being the most noteworthy exception, with a long history of adequately protecting depositors' balances as well as their privacy.

While we have already seen examples of how regulations can be used to undermine privacy, the relationship of regulation to the preservation of depositor funds deserves further explanation. Other than expropriation (which can be viewed as the ultimate breach of financial privacy), a depositor's balances are subject to three potential risks: bank failure, banking *system* failure (called "systemic risk"), and inflation. The methods for managing all three risks will be profoundly altered in the age of digital money.

A variety of regulatory measures are typically used to protect debtors against *bank failure*. Many such measures require banks to provide information about themselves to allow potential depositors or independent evaluators to judge a bank's safety, principally in terms of the adequacy of its capital base. In more sophisticated markets, bank supervision requirements have gone well beyond the publication of balance sheets and income statements and the calculation of ratios based upon them. In the case of banks, balance sheets and income statements can hide more than they reveal.

Risk-adjusted capital requirements,[106] first promulgated in the late 1980s under the auspices of the Bank for International Settlements, represent a major, if necessarily imperfect, step in the direction of relating the *quality* of a bank's assets to its capital funds. Such regulations are in the interest of bank depositors, and one can expect that banks adhering to the risk-adjusted capital standards will be at a strong competitive advantage in the digital age. Moreover, faced with the loss of formerly captive markets, many banks will seek to exceed required reporting and capital standards in order to assure depositors of their stability compared to their competitors worldwide.

Deposit insurance is the other frequently used measure to protect depositors from losses from bank failure. Unlike reporting and capital adequacy requirements, deposit insurance reimburses depositors *after* a bank has failed. Superfi-

---

[106]In a risk-adjusted system, a bank is required to maintain a level of capital funds that is a function of both the quality and size of the bank's asset portfolio.

cially, deposit insurance appears to be in the interest of all depositors, who will continue to demand a high level of protection in a competitive world market for banking services. Yet this is true only if insurance is provided to depositors at little or no incremental cost through a subsidized system, as is the case in many countries today. Of course *someone* must pay the costs, which in government-mandated systems principally means taxpayers.

Where deposit insurance is heavily subsidized by government, depositors' demands for insurance coverage will be limited only by the total amounts of their deposits. Some money will even be diverted from other investments to increase bank deposits beyond the level that would have been achieved in the absence of subsidized deposit insurance. This was clearly demonstrated in the United States in the early 1980s, when weak savings and loan associations (S&Ls), desperate for cash to fund their long-term asset portfolios, bid deposit rates to levels that were often higher than their yields on loans and higher than expected returns on most comparable investment alternatives. Because the first $100,000 of deposits was insured by a government agency at little marginal cost to the depositors (and the modest costs that were passed on did not distinguish risky from safe institutions), they had no incentive to seek safe S&Ls in which to place their funds and every incentive to shop for the highest deposit rates, regardless of the health of the offerors of those rates. Moreover, inappropriately-priced deposit insurance permitted S&Ls to take greater risks than they could have in the absence of insurance and to do so *without diminishing their capacity to attract deposits*. These are examples of the perverse incentives that economists collectively term "moral hazard."

Deposit insurance subsidies can be paid in a number of possible forms, principally:

1. through the assumption of unremunerated risk by taxpayers who involuntarily underwrite government insurance agencies;
2. through the payment by taxpayers of depositor indemnities that exceed the reserves of the insurance agency; or
3. through the recapitalization by taxpayers of insolvent banks.

The latter two subsidies, which entail cash outlays and not just incurring the risk of cash outlays, can be paid with explicit taxes on income or wealth or through a hidden tax on the savings of all citizens in the form of inflation of the money supply. This is a classic case of unprincipled politicians exploiting unscrupulously a flaw in representative democracy by which the benefits of a subsidy can be concentrated among an advantaged few who have the economic incentive to lobby for it, while the costs are dispersed among a much larger number who have little economic incentive to lobby in opposition. Ironically, the moral hazard that accompanies subsidized deposit insurance induces banks and depositors to take what would otherwise be imprudent risks, thereby greatly increasing the probability of bank failures which would trigger insurance payments.

In the world of digital money, deposit insurance subsidies will be difficult to sustain. As depositors increasingly ignore national boundaries, politicians will see little incentive to continue subsidies to foreigners who cannot vote for them. (With some mischievous glee, we can contemplate their opponents' demagogic attacks on subsidies to "rich foreigners.") Nationalists may be tempted to promote a variety of subsidized deposit insurance by which domestic but not foreign depositors are covered. This will prove uncompetitive as potential uninsured foreign depositors will recognize the moral hazard to which the most heavily subsidized of these banks are subject and will choose to place their money elsewhere. That is what happened in American savings and loans under comparable circumstances: few depositors maintained uninsured balances (those over $100,000) in suspect institutions, choosing rather to spread smaller deposits among a variety of S&Ls or, more significantly, to invest in alternatives (equities, mutual funds, real estate, etc.) that do not purport to insure against loss of principal.

Deposit insurance may still have a role to play when banking services are traded freely across international boundaries. Clearly, bank depositors consider deposit insurance to be of value, and some may be willing to pay an unsubsidized price for it in a free market. How many depositors will be willing to pay will depend upon their comparison of the value of such insurance with the price. Value is subjective, and each depositor will estimate it as a function of proposed interest rates, the depositor's perception of the risk of the bank and of the banking system in which it operates, and his willingness to accept risk. Most depositors will likely decide, quite rationally, to place their deposits in uninsured banks in which they are confident rather than pay for deposit insurance. Some banks will offer both insured and uninsured deposits at different rates. A depositor might also be able to engage insurance directly from the insurer rather than through a bank.

We can also expect to see the near disappearance of "zero-deductible" deposit insurance that reimburses 100% of the loss to an agreed maximum of coverage. Because such insurance increases the probability of bank failures, no insurer—other than an unwitting taxpayer!—would be foolish enough to offer it other than at a price that a foolish depositor would be willing to pay. (Of course, fools are not rare, and we can expect such insurance to be offered, quite harmlessly, in limited quantities and for banks of high quality.)

The norm will be partial coverage, with the depositor facing a tradeoff between insurance cost and the amount of any loss that he must bear. As with health insurance, we can expect to see insurance that covers 100% of a deposit after a deductible is met, insurance that covers a percentage of each loss (75 - 80% is a reasonable guess), and insurance that combines a deductible with a percentage reimbursement. While most insurance will likely be offered by private providers, governments in some countries will continue to offer the product, albeit with fewer subsidies. As in any free market, we can expect that a wide range of alternatives will be offered to depositors without burdening third parties.

Significantly, deposits in Swiss banks are not insured. They do not need to be. With its prudently managed banks of undoubted strength, its six decades of proven respect for financial privacy, and its hundreds of years of political stability, Switzerland and its banking system have no need to offer government deposit insurance to instill confidence among depositors. On the contrary, Swiss banking offers a model that increasingly will be adopted elsewhere.

It is in the control of *systemic risks* to the banking system that we find the most far-reaching regulatory implications of digital money. Systemic risks are those that have the potential to initiate a chain reaction provoking multiple bank failures and eventual collapse of the banking system. There are two general types of systemic crisis, characterized by either: 1) a contagion of bank *insolvency* accompanying a general economic crisis and usually associated with deflation, high rates of inflation, or currency depreciation; or 2) a contagion of bank *illiquidity* that spreads through the bank payments system. "Insolvency" is a fundamental problem characterized by the value of a bank's liabilities being greater than the value of its assets; *i.e.*, net worth is negative. "Illiquidity," by contrast, is normal among banks—much of their liabilities are payable upon demand, while most of their assets are not convertible to cash in a similarly short period. A bank may face an illiquidity crisis when higher than expected demand for cash by its depositors exceeds the liquid assets that the bank routinely maintains to meet normally anticipated demand.

The central banks of most countries seek to stem liquidity crises, which are viewed as temporary rather than fundamental in nature, through "lender-of-last-resort" (LLR) facilities by which they stand ready to prevent the spread of liquidity problems initially affecting only one or two banks. If a liquidity crisis is left unchecked, the presumption is that a general run on banks might be precipitated, culminating in a collapse of the banking system. This systemic risk results from the end-of-day settlements that characterize most payments systems: during the day the assets of the banking system are grossly inflated as banks incur liabilities to one another pending settlement at the close of business. (In some systems it is the central bank that incurs these intra-day liabilities, thereby directly underwriting systemic risks.) One bank's failure to meet its payment obligations at the end of the day can provoke a chain reaction of payment failures of other banks.

Unfortunately, in most countries, lender-of-last-resort facilities have been twisted into broad safety nets for insolvent banks, going far beyond the protection of the payments system from short-term liquidity problems. That LLR facilities are expected to save insolvent banks from the consequences of their own bad decisions is the single most destructive force undermining the health of banking systems. Banks are encouraged to take imprudent risks in the knowledge that they will be protected by their central banks and, ultimately, by the citizens in the form of high inflation and taxes. Eventually, the burdens become too great to sustain, and a banking crisis results to the detriment of all, including depositors. This is moral hazard in its most virulent form. The financial crises in Japan and Korea in 1997 and 1998 exemplify this problem.

Beginning in mid-1997, the world saw the results of a systemic bank crisis, which began in Thailand and then spread to Indonesia, South Korea, etc. and then on to Japan and Russia in 1998. The crisis began as a result of imprudent bank lending by both domestic and foreign banks in the affected countries. The IMF appears to have aggravated, rather than stopped, the crisis by giving international banks the impression that they would be the lenders of last resort (based on the precedent established during the Mexican financial crisis). In addition, at least initially, the IMF seems to have encouraged a round of competitive currency devaluations, which only made matters worse.

The good news is that digital money, and the attendant *de facto* removal of the geographic and legal barriers to depositors' exercise of free choice, will empower consumers to place their deposits conveniently in banks and banking systems that are prudently managed. Concomitantly, as with government deposit insurance schemes, politicians in countries with strong banking systems that are attractive to international depositors will see little incentive to underwrite those foreign deposits with a central bank's LLR facility. Countries will find it increasingly difficult to sustain unsound banking practices without seeing deposits flee to safer jurisdictions.

Moreover, thanks to advances in information technology, systemic risks to the payments system can be controlled without resorting to LLR facilities. A major step in this direction was taken by Switzerland in 1987, when it introduced a real time gross settlement system (RTGS) that eliminates the risk of a large, contagious end-of-day settlement failure. Settlements are effected continuously throughout the day, with no need for extensions of credit to the payments system by the central bank. The holding of reserves with the central bank was consequently made voluntary in Switzerland, with the result that reserve balances dropped by nearly 75% between 1988 and 1994, despite a substantial rise in daily payment

volumes.[107] Banks may choose to lend to each other during
the day, employing the same prudent standards by which they
lend to each other overnight. More recently, RTGS has been
adopted by the European Union countries.

The implications of real time settlement, in conjunction
with various forms of digital money and increasingly liquid
capital markets, are far-reaching. As systemic payments risk is
minimized, the payments system can be opened to a broad
range of participants employing electronic media of exchange.
In particular, when mutual funds gain direct access to the
payments system, the nature of banking itself will profoundly
change. "Banking" will no longer be limited to financial
institutions that undertake to redeem their deposit liabilities at
par. The value of the liabilities of a mutual fund bank will, as
with any mutual fund, always reflect the current value of its
assets. Most significantly, mutual funds are not subject to runs:
there is no incentive for mutual fund "depositors" to form a
queue to redeem investments whose value is continuously
marked to market. (By contrast, as mentioned earlier, when a
bank is subject to serious adverse rumors, justified or not,
bank depositors quite rationally seek to redeem their deposits
as soon as possible: redemption will either be at par or, after
the money runs out, at zero).

Let's imagine the ultimate manifestation of a mutual fund
banking system. To pay for goods or services, the buyer offers
a smart card issued by a mutual fund of his choice. The
seller's point-of-sale terminal (or computer in the case of a
transaction in cyberspace) immediately communicates through
the clearing system with the buyer's mutual fund, confirming
the buyer's payment instruction and the seller's instruction to
transfer funds to the mutual fund of *his* choice. There is
virtually no float in the system, with the buyer's assets working

---

[107]F. X. Browne and David Cronin, "Payments Technologies, Financial Innovation and Laissez
Faire Banking," Cato Journal, (Vol. 15, No. 1, Spring/Summer 1995), 110-112.

for him to the moment of the transaction, and the seller's assets earning a return from that moment forward. The assets of the buyer's fund effectively become the medium of exchange.

Today's par value banking model is in any case inappropriate for many of the situations to which it is applied. The commitment of a bank to redeem its deposits at par presumes a very conservative portfolio on the asset side of its balance sheet. This commitment is sustainable in relatively wealthy, developed market economies where there is a wide range of such conservative assets available to the banker. By contrast, financing needs in most emerging market countries generally entail high risks.

Not surprisingly, it is in these countries that lender-of-last-resort facilities and deposit insurance have been the most thoroughly destructive: banks are induced to assume equity risks disguised as loans, while undertaking to redeem their deposits at par. This is a no-lose situation for the so-called "bankers." If all goes well (which will initially appear to be the case, given that bad loans usually are bombs with long fuses), they reap high rewards; when their assets turn sour, others pick up the bill. Fortunately, in a classic case of technological leap, some emerging market countries, such as Russia, Estonia, and the Czech Republic, are rapidly adopting electronic money technologies, more so than many developed countries, while simultaneously encouraging the development of domestic capital markets that will support the establishment of mutual funds.

Thanks to technological innovation, banking is becoming more global and more competitive, while the risks of financial institutions and banking systems are becoming more manageable. Savers will increasingly find themselves empowered to achieve safety and privacy under regulatory systems that support rather than undermine those worthy objectives.

Chapter VII

TAXATION IN THE DIGITAL AGE

Nothing is certain except death and taxes, Benjamin Franklin said. But, the death of a tax is both rare and enjoyable. Enjoyment and liberation are coming, because the digital revolution is about to cause the death of most taxes on capital. What governments cannot see they cannot tax and, as a result of the digital revolution, the government will only see financial capital which is voluntarily revealed.

In order to understand what is about to happen, remember that the revolution taking place in electronic money means that banks and other organizations will be able to create their own money for transactional or investment purposes and literally move these monies around the globe at the speed of light. The definition of money as a government-created legal tender will become less and less relevant. The existing distinctions between money, goods, services and assets will dwindle as they become more interchangeable.

When the definition of money becomes blurred, things which can be transformed instantaneously into something else, and moved to anyplace in the world with no paper or electronic trail, will become nearly impossible to tax. By using public key cryptography, one can have electronic bank notes certified without the issuer knowing to whom they were issued. Also, as previously noted, smart cards used as an electronic purse can have the same anonymity as paper cash.

Government authorities cannot stop this revolution because it is global, and too many people throughout the world now have the knowledge. Censorship and regulation will not work, because those who are developing the means of evasion will always be far ahead of those who are trying to restrict it. Increasingly, clever people go to work for computer software and hardware companies rather than government agencies, because that is where the action and the money are. Why be stifled in a government bureaucracy which has as its goal to regulate or restrain your fellow citizens when you can be in the private sector creating products that both liberate and enhance the lives of mankind?

In the same way that most totalitarian governments (with the exception of China, North Korea, Cuba, and a few others) have largely given up trying to completely control the flow of information, because technology has made it a fruitless task, government officials need to realize that the old central bank monopolies on the issuance of money will also go the way of the buggy whip. Government officials have two choices: to redesign their tax and monetary systems to reflect technological reality; or to try to create a system in which every investment and every expenditure by every person is known. In the new world of digital freedom there is no halfway ground because, if any privacy is granted, all sensitive information can be hidden in that same digital "drawer." A government which attempts to be all-knowing is doomed to failure, practically and politically. Nevertheless, attempts to impose a "big brother" government can slow down the benefits of the digital age, while trampling the liberties of the people.

What Can Be Taxed in the Digital Age

Only what can be taxed efficiently should be taxed at all. If taxpayers may easily avoid reporting particular types of income or transactions, with virtually no danger of being caught because of technological innovations, then the tax becomes, quite literally, voluntary. The tax is voluntary when it is only paid by those conscientious citizens who abide by the tax laws out of a sense of duty and honor rather than the threat of civil or criminal penalties.

The tax base (*i.e.*, what is taxed) of the future will not include financial capital (*i.e.*, productive savings), because financial capital too easily can become invisible. The future tax base will have to rely on real and tangible property, payments by institutions to individuals and other institutions, and payments for tangible goods. As capital taxation declines, user fees for government services will increase as a percentage of total government revenue.

Taxes tied to real property or tangible personal property or the sale of goods and services to the public are much more difficult to evade. Taxes tied to the employer-employee relationship (with the exception of domestic workers—"the nanny tax") are enforceable because of the stability, length and visibility of the relationship. (However, this is not true for employees in remote locations or in the sovereign areas of another government). Taxes tied to the operation of businesses dealing with the public or with many business customers are more easily enforced because of the necessarily public and open nature of such businesses.

As noted earlier, it is the nearly instantaneous encrypted nature of financial transactions that makes taxation of capital transactions[108] problematic. The cost of trying to enforce the taxation of financial capital probably will exceed the revenue collected and certainly will exact a price in terms of lost efficiency and lost privacy rights that exceeds the benefits of their continued taxation. The good news is that in the future, as the tax burden on capital declines, higher rates of economic growth and higher real incomes for most people are likely to occur.

Taxing capital is equivalent to destroying the "seed corn" of the economy. In the modern economy, businesses must "save" enough, above what they pay out in wages, expenses, and dividends to stockholders, to buy new equipment and pay for research and development, if the business is to prosper in the future. When the government taxes business profits, the business has less to invest in new equipment and research and development. This directly translates into lower productivity growth, which in turn means lower real economic growth, and a slower growth in personal incomes. When the government taxes an individual's interest receipts, dividends, and capital gains, it both discourages that individual from saving and reduces the amount of money that individual can invest in productive activities.

Even though good economists have long known that it is counter-productive to tax capital heavily—that is, corporate profits, capital gains, interest and dividends—the US and many other countries have continued to do it. The reason is the political appeal of appearing to tax the rich. Some rich people earn most of their income from capital gains, interest and dividends, so it seems only natural to put a hefty tax on them. Such reasoning ignores the fact that the income which pro-

---

[108]including interest, dividends, and capital gains.

duces those capital gains, interest, and dividends has already been taxed at least once if not more, and that lower income people would be the greatest beneficiaries of lower taxes on capital. Lowering the taxes on capital "frees up" money that can be allocated to other purposes. This extra money can then be spent to expand businesses and hire more employees.[109]

Taxation of capital also destroys upward mobility because potential entrepreneurs are denied the opportunity to better themselves due to the artificial "capital shortage." It is hypocritical for politicians who have inherited wealth to propose and enact higher taxes on capital gains—which is a tax on getting wealthy as opposed to being wealthy.

Capital investment creates jobs. How many truck drivers would there be if there were no trucks? Countries that have little capital have high unemployment rates and low incomes. Countries that have lots of capital and capital investment have close to full employment and high incomes.

The US taxation of capital is relatively high compared to that of consumption, hence it imports (borrows) capital from countries that tax consumption more heavily and capital less heavily, which is why the US has a trade deficit. Those who wish to invest in the US because of its economic and political stability and relatively high rate of return on capital need dollars to invest. The way they obtain dollars is by selling Americans a good or service. If foreigners did not want dollars, America would not have a trade deficit.

If the US had lower taxes on capital, Americans would save more and thus borrow less from foreigners. This in turn would lower the US trade deficit and increase the rate of

---

[109]For more information about this, check out the International Policy Institute's website at http://www.ipi.org.

domestic investment, leading to higher real incomes.[110] Privatizing Social Security would have the benefits of not only protecting the retirement nest eggs of younger people, but, by reducing the tax on labor and capital, would spur economic growth and raise the national saving level.

The need for fundamental tax reform is now obvious to all—except for a few politicians, tax lawyers and accountants who have a vested interest in complexity and selective enforcement. Despite widespread agreement that fundamental changes are needed in the tax system, there is little agreement as to how to change it. Economists are concerned with improving its efficiency, and most would shift the burden away from taxing labor and capital (what people put into the economy) towards taxing consumption (what people take out of the economy).

There is a general acknowledgment that the US tax system has reached a complexity which is not only unmanageable for the average citizen, but for the tax professional as well. Every April, a story appears in one or more of the business and financial publications, demonstrating that tax professionals are incapable of calculating the correct amount of tax for some hypothetical, middle-income taxpayer, who does not have an unduly complex situation. Typically, income and spending details of the hypothetical taxpayer are provided to a number of the leading tax preparation firms and several IRS offices, and each tax professional is asked to calculate the tax owed. As would be expected, each tax professional comes up with a different answer, and each IRS office comes up with a different answer. All of this would be amusing if it were not for the fact that you, Mr. or Ms. Taxpayer, could go to jail for the

[110]Readers who are interested in the taxation of capital should contact the American Council for Capital Formation, for studies and references. They may be reached at info@accf.org, or at 1750 K Street, NW, Suite 400, Washington, DC 20006-2302, Tel. (202) 293-5811. Their Internet home page is: http://www.accf.org.

wrong answer, even if the wrong answer is provided by your accountant.

This is exactly what happened to New York hotelier Leona Helmsley. Mrs. Helmsley had two things going against her. She was very rich and reputed not to be a nice lady, "the queen of the mean." She was accused of saying that "only the little people pay taxes," although she denied it. She actually paid a lot of taxes, but her alleged comment made her a prime target for the IRS—they got her, and off to prison she went. She may or may not have been trying to cheat the IRS, but it is clear she was targeted. Her case was another victory for selective law enforcement.[111] You might recall that when Bill and Hillary Clinton underpaid their taxes, they merely paid the amount owed plus interest. No jail sentence, no public condemnation for the Clintons. So much for equality under the law.

Fortunately, the American people have showed their displeasure with tax punishment roulette by electing people to Congress who are serious about getting rid of much of the complexity. House Majority Leader Dick Armey, a former professor of economics, has developed a flat tax, and the Chairman of the House Ways and Means Committee, Bill Archer, has developed a sales tax alternative. Both approaches would work better than the current tax code, but neither approach is yet adequately suited to the age of digital money.

A key ingredient in the success of any new tax system will be the rates—especially the marginal rate (*i.e.*, the rate that a

[111]"The Helmsleys were a cash cow for the IRS, paying $53.7 million in federal taxes on adjusted gross income of $103.6 million.

The government's claim that the Helmsleys underreported their income by $2.6 million in order to evade the $1.7 million in taxes implies that the Helmsleys would have noticed the difference between the $53.7 million they paid and the $55.4 million that the government claimed they owed." (from Paul Craig Roberts' article, "Leona May Be Guilty, but Not as Charged," <u>Wall Street Journal</u> 9 April 1992).

taxpayer pays on the last dollar of income, or the highest rate any taxpayer pays). The most successful tax systems have low marginal rates. If the rate is low enough, most people will pay it without much complaint and few will take steps to avoid it. On the other hand, high tax rate systems give huge rewards for tax evasion or avoidance. If the tax rate is 90%, then for every hundred dollars you can avoid reporting you get to keep an extra ninety—a big incentive. If the tax rate is only 10%, then for every hundred dollars you avoid reporting you only get to keep ten—no big deal, and certainly not one worth risking a fine or jail.

High tax rates cause people to find legal or illegal ways to avoid the tax, and they can always choose leisure (a non-taxed activity) over work (a taxed activity). In recent years, economists have increasingly studied the rate at which different types of taxes maximize tax revenue. The longer the time period, the lower the rate needs to be to maximize revenue, because people will adjust their behaviors over time to minimize the tax. For example, a tax rate of 100% on income will, over the long run, produce zero revenue, because no one will continue to work—or at least report the work and income. A customs tax or sales tax needs to be sufficiently low to keep people from smuggling the product or refusing to purchase it. As many will recall from American history, the British failed to maximize the tax revenue on tea in 1773, as evidenced by its trip to the bottom of Boston harbor rather than to the tables of the Colonists.

The relationship between tax rates and tax revenues is commonly referred to as the Laffer Curve, after Professor Arthur B. Laffer. The Laffer Curve demonstrates that there are two tax rates that produce the same amount of revenue—a high rate (negative) and a low rate (positive). Rates in the negative range (high rates) will increase revenue when they are reduced, and rates that are in the positive range (low rates) will increase revenue when they are increased. For instance, a very high tax rate on labor will discourage people from working (at least in the reported economy). By lowering the tax, people will take jobs and the tax revenue collected by the government will increase. As Professor Laffer and others have noted, the difference between tax revenues and tax rates has been understood by wise men for at least 4,000 years, but foolish politicians have yet to learn the lessons of the last 40 centuries.

Politicians (as well as some tax lawyers, accountants, and even economists) have a hard time learning that tax rates and tax revenues are not the same thing. At various times and various places, politicians have managed to destroy many legitimate industries and create criminal ones by overtaxing the legitimate ones. The Clinton Administration finally had to accept a less-qualified Attorney General who had no children because it could not seem to find its political ideal, a qualified married woman lawyer with children who had paid the "nanny tax." (The reason none of them had paid it is because it takes a great deal of time—and time is expensive for high-priced lawyers—to comply with a lot of paperwork for a minuscule tax.[112])

Will Tax Evasion Increase in the Age of Digital Money?

Many of those seeking to regulate digital money, smart cards, the Internet, etc. claim that if they do not regulate, tax avoidance and evasion will occur. As usual, those with the totalitarian mind-set miss the point. They are correct in their assertion that tax evasion and tax avoidance will increase— unless the tax laws are changed to reflect the digital reality. They are, however, wrong in their assertion that more regula-

---

[112]For more information about the economics of taxation, contact the Institute for Research of the Economics of Taxation (IRET), at Tel. (202) 463-1400 or 1300 19th Street, NW, Washington, DC 20036.

tion will succeed in coaxing much more tax revenue from unwilling payers. Again, the fact is that the digital revolution is going to make some tax evasion very easy, and if it is easy, increasing numbers of people will take advantage of it. If you can sit at home and, with a few key strokes on your computer, avoid paying the tax, the temptation to do so will be great.

Assume you are a lawyer in New York doing work for a client in a jurisdiction without an income tax. You do your work in New York but send it via the Internet (as electronic mail). The client agrees to pay you in electronic money. As your bills become due, the client sends the money to you over the Internet and it is downloaded into your computer. You, in turn, pay your bills by sending electronic cash from your computer and by loading up your smart card. And only you—a smart New York lawyer—decide what electronic and paper records both to create and keep. Anyone who can sell his personal services over the Internet—lawyers, programmers, writers, architects, and engineers, for example—will have the same ability.[113]

In the digital age, it will be increasingly easy to move or create a financial portfolio anywhere in the world, and to do it in an anonymous and encrypted way. Many people will clearly choose to do so.

The government can respond in two ways: it can try to know and control everything (the totalitarian response); or it can adapt its rules to the new reality (the libertarian or classical liberal response). (A middle course is impossible since it would lead to thoroughgoing corruption and civil struggle). For those readers who are uncertain as to the right course of action, remember that Hitler, Marx, and Stalin would have

[113]This example is drawn from "The New Monetary Universe and Its Impact on Taxation," by Richard W. Rahn, and published in The Future of Money in the Information Age, edited by James A. Dorn, 1997.

likely given the totalitarian response, and Jefferson, Franklin, and Madison likely would have given the libertarian response. Some will view the previous statements as heavy-handed and overkill, which they are—but they are also true. It says something about one's character as to whose intellectual company one chooses to keep.

When Is Tax Evasion Morally Justified?

An argument against financial privacy is that it will make the collection of some types of taxes more difficult for governments. This argument is indeed true, but that is not a justification for preventing financial privacy; in fact, it can be an argument for *protecting* financial privacy. When a government is unjust and corrupt, the people have both the right and duty to oppose it. A form of opposition is the refusal to fund the government to the best of one's ability, which can take the form of deliberate tax avoidance or evasion.

The statutes of many countries, including the US, make it illegal to fund or make payments to criminal organizations. But what if the government is the criminal organization? The National Socialist (Nazi) government under Hitler was, by any definition, a criminal organization. The true patriots and friends of freedom in Germany were those Germans, Jews and others, who found means by which to move their financial capital out of Germany to presumed safe havens. No one faults them for evading German taxes, because clearly any tax receipts or confiscation of financial assets by the Nazi government were likely to be used, in part, for immoral and corrupt purposes, including funding the concentration camps, and for offensive weapons of mass destruction. In Hitler's Germany, the moral person was the tax evader.

The twentieth century is littered with the skeletons of

criminal governments that were funded by the taxes of their own citizens. To the extent that people were able to deny such governments funds, lives were saved.

The question of the right and moral course of actions when one is confronted with a Hitler is easy, but what if one is confronted with a democratically-elected government which is corrupt, but not criminal in the Hitlerian sense? For example, the local government in the District of Columbia (Washington) was, by any reasonable definition, a very corrupt government under its former Mayor, Marion Barry.[114] Because of the incompetence and corruption, the citizens and visitors to the City did not receive even a small fraction of what they paid for. Instead, they received an often corrupt and incompetent police force with a miserable success rate in solving crimes; a school system which spent far more than the national average per pupil and yet failed to provide many of them with a basic education; a contracting system operated to reward friends of the mayor; a self-indulgent bureaucracy which felt little need to serve its citizens; and so on. Some residents of the District of Columbia developed elaborate schemes for evading DC taxes which they were legally obligated to pay. When people begin deciding for themselves which taxes to pay and not pay, the very institution of government is undermined.

Next door to the District of Columbia, there is Fairfax

[114]Examples of this corruption abound. The Washington Post reports that the District of Columbia's Water and Sewer Authority's workers have been moonlighting making plumbing repairs on private homes using the city's equipment on city time, abandoning their daily work assignments. This, at least, when they were working at all. Washington Post staff writer Michael Powell also took up Mayor Barry's challenge to "see the results of their [city employees'] work" and reported on what he found. The Washington Post printed an editorial with the following summary of his findings:

Reporter Powell also spent five days covertly trailing a pair of five-man D.C. Water and Sewer Authority work crews around the city. What's that about the mayor's invitation to "observing and see the results of their work?" Over five days, The Post's reporter did just that. He saw one crew work for one hour the first day and perform no work whatever the next day. The other crew that he observed spent no more than four hours working on one day and performed no work at all on another day. [From the editorial, "Soaking D.C. Taxpayers," Washington Post, 20 December 1997. A20.]

County, Virginia. Fairfax County is widely regarded as well-managed and honest, delivering a high quality of services (at least by government standards) at not excessive costs to its citizens. Not all the citizens agree with all of the spending the County engages in but, given the democratic nature of the government and the lack of corruption and mismanagement, a citizen of Fairfax would find little moral justification for evading taxes lawfully due.

Unfortunately, not all governments are run as honestly and competently as Fairfax County in the State of Virginia. To maintain a civilized society, it is important for people to believe that their governmental units are honest and reasonably efficient. People who believe that their government is corrupt will find the moral justification for "opting out" of tax payments if they think they can get away with it. The correct policy is to promote honest and efficient government, such as that found in Virginia and Switzerland, not more totalitarian tax enforcement. The American experience shows that most people will pay their taxes if, on balance, they believe they will be well spent.

What Is the Optimum Size of Government?

That government is best which governs least.

—Henry David Thoreau

The reductions in the tax base and tax rates that will be required in the digital age will by necessity make the relative size of government smaller. Fortunately, the required relative shrinking of government was something that needed to be done anyway if mankind was to reach its full economic, social and personal potential.

Historically, government spending had been a relatively small share of GDP in most countries. It was only with the rise of the Marxists, socialists, and Keynesians in the first half of the twentieth century that an ever-growing government sector was viewed as desirable. As a result, in most countries, total government spending as a percent of GDP has grown rapidly and continuously in this century.[115]

By the 1970s and 1980s, it had become obvious to many economists that economic growth was suffering from the rapid increase in taxation and expenditure on the part of government. It is now widely acknowledged that government is often the problem rather than the solution, and that government often makes people worse off rather than better off. The collapse of communism and the growing disenchantment with and loss of respectability of socialism and Keynesianism are evidence of the loss of faith in government solutions. The traditional parties of the left are moving right. The British Labour party formally rejected socialism as part of its platform and then proceeded to victory. The leader of America's party of the left, President Clinton, announced (at least for the record) that "the era of big government is over."

Despite the increasing calls for a rollback, government in most places is not dramatically shrinking, in part because the advocates of smaller government do not agree on "how small" government should be. During the past twenty years there have been many studies indicating that much of the current government spending and taxing is counterproductive.[116]

---

[115]A recent study by Vito Tanzi and Ludger Schuknecht of the International Monetary Fund has documented this growth of government. They show that, in the OECD countries, total government spending as a percentage of GDP rose from an average of 8.3% in 1870 to 47.2% in 1994.

[116]Several studies have been done that illustrate these findings. The following is a list of some recent studies that show the relationship between the size of government and economic growth.

Fox, Harrison, and Richard W. Rahn, "What is the Optimum Size of Government," Sponsored by the Krieble Foundation, 1996.

Marsden, Keith. "Links Between Taxes and Economic Growth: Some Empirical Evidence," *Journal of Economic Growth*, Volume 1 Number 4 (Fourth Quarter 1986).

Most studies of the relationship between economic growth and government spending have found negative correlations for most countries for most time periods—that is, big government impedes economic growth. Despite these strong empirical findings, some economic textbooks and economists still argue that government spending promotes economic growth. This view is the foundation of the Keynesian macroeconomic tradition, which became dominant during the Great Depression.[117]

Many economists were reluctant from the beginning to accept the basic Keynesian alchemy that a modest increase in the level of government expenditure could result in a dramatic expansion of the national economy; that is, that it is possible to get something for nothing. Fortunately, Keynesian economics is now largely discredited. The new classical economists, along with monetarists, supply-siders, public choicers, Austrians, *et al.*, have successfully refuted the Keynesian preoccupation with demand while ignoring supply and the adverse consequences of government taxing and spending.

Robbins, Gary and Aldona. "Capital, Taxes and Growth" *NCPA Policy Report* No. 169. January 1992.

Scully, Gerald W. "What is the Optimal Size of Government in the United States?" *NCPA Policy Report* No. 188. November 1994.

Grossman, Philip J. "Government and Economic Growth: A Non-linear Relationship" *Public Choice.* Vol. 56 (1988).

Landau, Daniel. "Government and Economic Growth in the Less Developed Countries: An Empirical Study for 1960-1980." *Economic Development and Cultural Change.* Vol. 35 (October 1986).

Marlow, Michael L. "Private Sector Shrinkage and the Growth of Industrialized Economies." *Public Choice.* Vol. 49 (1986).

Rahn, Richard W., Cesar Conda, and William Orzechowski. "Economic Growth and Government Spending." (working paper) US Chamber of Commerce, Economic Policy Division. (1986).

Barth, James R. and Michael D. Bradley. "The Impact of Government Spending on Economic Activity." Department of Economics, George Washington University. National Chamber Foundation (Summer 1987).

[117] According to Keynesian theory, business cycles are directly related to weaknesses in the demand side of the economy. Therefore, in order to mitigate the effects of depressions, Keynesians recommend that the government adopt fiscal policies to manage demand. The theory is that since government expenditure is a significant accounting component of demand, it is possible for the government to stimulate demand by increasing spending. If the economy has sufficient excess capacity, which is the case during recessions, the increased demand caused by government expenditure will spur corresponding increases in production to meet the new level of demand. In other words, Keynesian theory reduced to its elements asserts that if the government looks after demand, supply will take care of itself.

What Keynesians overlooked is that government expenditure also entails a plethora of costs, including extraction costs. Public spending means a reduction in private spending or private investment and is likely, on balance, to be less efficient in allocating resources across the economy. Public spending also frequently establishes disincentives to work, save, and invest. All of these costs reduce the national income.

The government has three basic ways to finance public spending: taxation, borrowing, or printing money (which is taxation in the form of inflation). Public spending financed by printing money may increase nominal income but will have little effect on real income because the supply of resources in the economy is unchanged, even though the supply of money is increased. When the government taxes or borrows, however, it extracts resources out of the private sector of the economy. Keynesians policies largely ignore the fact that this extraction of resources is costly. Economists who have analyzed the cost of extracting funds to finance public spending have demonstrated that this expense represents a significant share of national income.

Extraction is costly to the extent that individuals dislike transferring their income to the government. For example, suppose the government decides to finance expenditure by raising marginal tax rates on income. An individual deciding whether to work an additional hour now finds that the after-tax return for the extra work is lower, or alternatively that the opportunity cost of not working the extra hour—that is, the cost of enjoying an hour of leisure—is now lower. Since leisure is a good, economic theory predicts that, holding all else constant, as the expense of leisure falls as a result of rising marginal tax rates, individuals will consume more leisure. Hence, they will work less (at least in the taxed sector), thereby reducing national income.

For government expenditure to increase income, therefore, the increase in income produced by public spending must more than offset the reduction in income caused by the way the expenditure is financed. The real cost of government expenditures is significantly higher than costs that show up on the budget. In addition to the rise in government expenditures, individuals and businesses incur substantial compliance costs when they are required to maintain records and to calculate their respective tax liabilities. The Report of the President's Council of Economic Advisors in 1985 noted a study that found the average compliance cost of Federal and State personal income taxes to be between five and seven percent of the revenue that such taxes raise.

A number of economists have estimated the economic effect of government expenditures on the supply side of the economy. These studies show that government expenditures reduce economic growth rates not only because extraction costs are substantial, but also because many kinds of government expenditures have a negative effect on economic growth that is completely separate from the cost of extraction. The key to understanding how public spending by itself reduces income is to understand that not all government expenditure has the same effect on the economy. (For greater detail, see the studies listed in footnote 116.)

Government expenditure is comprised of three basic components: transfer payments, purchases of goods and services, and investment spending. Each type of government expenditure is likely to have different effects on output. Of the three components, investment spending is the only expenditure that might lead to greater output. Transfer payments, which require that an individual stop undertaking productive activity in order to qualify, reduce rather than expand economic output. For example, individuals will lose Social Security payments if they work and earn more than some threshold level. Welfare recipients in most cases will lose government benefits if they engage in full employment. Thus, transfer payments often provide disincentives for individuals to be productive. Governmental purchases of goods and services only replace private consumption and do not increase income.

At very low levels of government spending, economic growth is also low. In conditions of anarchy or weak government, the public goods and services essential for the proper functioning of markets—personal property rights, police forces to protect the rights of people and property, an effective judicial system, national defense against foreign predations, etc.—simply do not exist.

Once government provides essential public goods (a public good is an indivisible benefit, like constitutional rights or national defense, that government alone can provide and can provide only to all citizens), it becomes possible for government spending to weaken the economy. That is because government, if it continues to grow, inevitably begins to duplicate services provided by the private sector. Because the government has the power to grant itself a legal monopoly or oligopoly, it can prevent private firms from competing and can run enterprises on the basis of political, as opposed to economic, considerations.

A variety of factors, including the type of spending, undoubtedly influences the level at which government spending becomes counterproductive. Basic infrastructure payments, for instance, generally help the economy. Subsidies of all varieties do not. What is indisputable is that the greater the level of government spending, the greater the chances that it will be put to less-than-optimal use. Public choice economists have established the behavioral theory for explaining this phenomenon.

Why We Have More Government than We Want

*A government which robs Peter to pay Paul
can always depend on the support of Paul.*

—George Bernard Shaw

As government spending grows and the number of beneficiaries increases, politicians begin showering money on distinct
constituencies. Expensive federal income transfer and cash
assistance programs, such as farm subsidies and mass transit,
help small groups of people while weakening the economy
generally. Thus, many well-meaning social programs have
adverse effects on savings and labor supply because they
discourage productive activity. These all are the natural result
of political incentives. Politicians get "paid"—re-elected—for
directing government money toward their constituents, or
providing them with special tax privileges.

Politicians usually support the growth of bigger government
by increasing taxes. The combination of high levels of government spending and the associated high tax burdens necessary
to finance that spending effectively deprive the productive
private sector of much needed capital. Thus, as government
gets more "successful," an economy can get increasingly weak.

Public choice theory explains that unless properly con-
strained, governments have a natural proclivity to grow. Welfare economics has shown that the marginal excess burden
from raising new tax revenue is often higher than the return
from any conceivable new government program. The result is
that economic growth rates will inevitably decline as the naturally expanding government adopts new spending programs
with revenue extracted from over-taxed, income-producing
activities and assets owned by private citizens.

Chapter VIII

SURVIVING THE TRANSITION TO DIGITAL MONEY

*I do not think it is an exaggeration to say that it is wholly im-
possible for a central bank subject to political control,
or even exposed to serious political pressure, to regulate
the quantity of money in a way conducive to a smoothly
functioning market order. A good money, like good law,
must operate without regard to the effect that decisions
of the issuer will have on known groups or individuals.
A benevolent dictator might conceivably disregard these
effects; no democratic government dependent on a
number of special interests can possibly do so.*

—F. A. Hayek[118]

In 1976, Friedrich Hayek wrote the first edition of <u>Dena-
tionalization of Money</u>. (Hayek who, in the judgment of
many, was the greatest economist of the twentieth century, had
already won the Nobel Prize in economics.) The book argued
that the monopolization of money by government was neither

---

[118]F.A. Hayek, <u>Denationalization of Money</u>, 3d ed., The Institute of Economic Affairs
(Lancing, Sussex: Goron Pro-Print Co Ltd., 1990), 117-118.

necessary nor desirable, and raised many eyebrows when it was first published. During the ensuing two decades, Hayek's proposals have gone from an intellectual curiosity to a major part of the field of "new monetary economics." Like so much of Hayek's earlier work, his advocacy of private competitive currencies based on a market basket of commodities was ahead of its time.[119]

Hayek had carefully described how private competitive currencies could come about and why they were vastly superior to the existing government-monopoly monetary order. He was well aware of the resistance governments and central banks would put up to avoid losing the power and profit that comes from being the monopoly provider of money. At the end of Denationalization of Money, Hayek wrote:

> What is now urgently required is not the construction of a new system but the prompt removal of all the legal obstacles which have for two thousand years blocked the way for an evolution which is bound to throw up beneficial results which we cannot now foresee.[120]

---

[119]In 1984, at a meeting of the Mont Pelerin Society in Cambridge, England, I had a conversation with Hayek, during which he told me that he had been invited by the Chicago Mercantile Exchange to discuss with them the possibility of establishing a commodity basket futures contract to act as a surrogate money for inflation protection. He was very enthusiastic about the upcoming trip, even though he was in his mid-eighties at the time. Having been a fan of Hayek's proposal, I had made a similar proposal to The New York Mercantile Exchange (for whom I had done some work) several years earlier. The President of the Exchange, Richard Levine, liked the idea but explained to me that his board, primarily composed of commodity traders, had a short view of the long run (i.e., the next five minutes), and hence was unenthusiastic. I told Professor Hayek of my experience, and cautioned him to keep his expectations low. Several months later, I happened to see him in Washington, and I asked him about the Chicago trip. He laughed and indicated that his experience had been similar to mine. During our earlier conversation in Cambridge, in describing the reasons for his own ultimate success in his modest and amusing way, he said, "Remember young man, part of the key to success is outliving your enemies." Hayek not only lived to see the intellectual triumph of his school of economics over that of his old friend and nemesis Keynes, but also to see the collapse of communism, whose evils he had so vividly described in 1944 in his best-selling book, The Road to Serfdom, and whose demise he so accurately predicted in his last book, The Fatal Conceit.

[120]F. A. Hayek, Denationalization of Money, 3d ed., The Institute of Economic Affairs (Lancing, Sussex: Goron Pro-Print Co Ltd., 1990), 134.

. What Hayek did not foresee in 1976, nor did anyone else, is how a combination of technologies twenty years later would enable an end run around the forces of monopoly and inertia. Again, to review, those technologies that will make Hayek's ideal not only a possibility but a reality are:

- *The Internet*–for it establishes the communication system which can be accessed by all on a global basis and which is now outside the control of any one political entity.

- *The Semiconductor Chip*–which, as described in Moore's Law, doubles in power every eighteen months, enabling any individual to access the large amount of computing power necessary to move data, including money, anywhere in the world quickly in encrypted form.

- *Public Key Encryption*–which enables anyone to communicate with anyone else on the globe with a degree of privacy that cannot be breached by governments without extreme efforts.

- *Global Commodities Futures Markets*– which enable anyone on the globe to know the price of any freely-traded currency or any specific commodity, such as gold, or of a defined market basket of goods and services at any time.

- *Asset Securitization*–enabling many assets to serve as the backing for private monies.

- *Smart Cards*–which provide an easy and convenient way to store, dispense and collect electronic money (*i.e.*, to buy and sell) outside both the electronic communications systems and banking systems when it is desired or when it is necessary.

+ *Very Low Cost Telecommunications*—As
technology futurist George Gilder has pro-
claimed, "The law of the telecosm ordains
that the total bandwidth of communications
systems will triple every year for 25 years."[121]
What this means is that global communications will get less and less expensive, and
thus electronic money will be increasingly
less expensive to both hold and use in transactions.

These technologies working in concert mean Digital
Liberation. Bits operating to perform the functions of
money can be placed almost anywhere on the globe at almost
anytime in a few minutes, without the knowledge of any
government or anyone who is not a direct party to the transaction.

Most data, including money, will be transmitted by fiber
optic lines, because, "one fiber thread could carry 25 times
more bits than last year's [1996] average traffic load of all the
world's communications networks put together: an estimated
terabit (trillion bits) per second."[122] In addition to fiber optic
lines, other technologies, such as low orbit satellites, are becoming more widespread. This enables individuals with
pocket communicators to operate directly to and from the
satellite. Thus, people will have access to the Internet anywhere on the globe, even where there are no wires.

Because the technological problems have been or are now
being solved, private money is on its way; and no government
is going to be able to stop its arrival or its flow. Concealing
one's financial transactions will be easy for those who wish to

---

[121]George Gilder, "Fiber Keeps its Promise," Forbes: ASAP, 7 April 1997, 92.
[122]Ibid.

do so, and governmental efforts to make private money illegal or taxable will ultimately fail.

Individuals versus Government

A government above the law is a menace to be defeated.

Lord Scarman[123]

In the past, if the government failed to protect the person and property of the individual, or became the oppressor, people had little choice but to endure and submit, or revolt. The digital age changes the balance between governmental power and individual rights, in that it will be increasingly easy for people largely to "opt out" if they are dissatisfied with a government.

The very wealthy have been opting out for years. When Swedish tax rates became oppressive (in some cases more than 100%) in the 1960s and 1970s, several high profile film stars, entrepreneurs, and other leading citizens left the country and became tax refugees. Many countries now offer citizenship or permanent residency to the rich in exchange for an agreement for a certain fixed tax payment each year, as in the case of Switzerland, or an agreement to bring in a stipulated amount of investment and/or an agreement to create a certain number of new jobs, as in the case of the US and Canada. A number of small nations have created a virtual industry in attracting the rich by offering tax breaks. (Many of the OECD countries feel threatened by these developments and are arguing for common action to stop "harmful tax competition.") Certain Swiss cantons will negotiate with individuals meeting certain criteria

---

[123]Lord Scarman was a British judge. Qtd. in The Oxford Dictionary of Political Quotations, (ed. Antony Jay, Oxford: Oxford University Press, 1996).

(*i.e.*, foreigners who have never lived in Switzerland) special tax arrangements based on the taxpayers' estimated expenses, but independent of their worldwide income. Such arrangements are unlikely to be lower than $50,000 and are generally much higher. However, they can result in a low tax rate for very high income individuals. In the United Kingdom, a similar and very successful status exists for foreigners deemed "non-domiciled residents," who are only taxed on their UK-sourced income. The US, Canada and many other countries have established programs to attract high net worth individuals by offering to give them permanent residency in exchange for certain levels of investment. The US program has not worked well, because the amount of required investment is too high ($1 million), and the investor is subject to US worldwide taxation. Some Caribbean island nations will provide a passport and permanent residency for a one-time payment of an amount as small as $50,000.

As noted earlier, in the digital world it becomes increasingly possible for those whose profession or occupation can be carried out over electronic media, such as the Internet, to live anywhere they so choose and still make a living. Why live in—and pay taxes in—a crowded, dirty, crime-ridden, high-tax city, if you can do your job equally well from a Caribbean island or from a Swiss ski resort?

Increasingly, governments are competing for individuals with skills and money. There are approximately two dozen countries (out of approximately two hundred separate political entities in the world) that offer various degrees of financial privacy for both their own citizens and foreigners. The number of political entities (separate countries or largely independent political entities) in the world has roughly tripled in the past fifty years—as a result of decolonization, the breaking up of such former empires as the Soviet Union, and other ethnic independence movements. This process is probably not over, and thus the world can expect to have more rather than fewer countries. Many of these new countries and semi-independent political entities are small in geographic size and/or population, and are seeking comparative advantages. The lessons of Hong Kong, Singapore, and the Cayman Islands have not been lost on many of these new countries. They understand that a quick way to attract the financial capital and highly-skilled people they need is to provide a climate of low taxes and financial privacy, coupled with a solid infrastructure and low crime.

The digital age makes it easier to attract these desirable, high-skilled, wealthy individuals, and to create industries, such as software production, that can be conducted over the Internet. The larger, high-tax, intrusive, regulation-prone countries will increasingly feel the competitive pressure. Some will reform their own governments to make them more citizen- and taxpayer-friendly, and others will become more restrictive in an attempt to stem the outflow of money and minds. The US government has been attempting to impose taxes on some so-called tax refugees who have left the country and renounced their American citizenship. When in the '80s the Soviet Union attempted to engage in similar actions (property seizures) against their citizens that had fled, Americans were justifiably outraged. There is more than a little hypocrisy here by some members of Congress and US tax officials.

Screams of disloyalty by demagogic politicians against those who opt out are likely to have little effect as long as tax and regulatory policies are perceived to be unfair by those who suffer under them. Many people will find it easy to morally justify evading taxes by moving assets to low- or non-tax jurisdictions as long as people feel they are paying an unfair portion of the total tax burden (the top 1% of the taxpayers, who have 14% of the income, pay 29% of the taxes in the

US[124]); see their hard-earned tax dollars spent in a wasteful or corrupt manner; are burdened with expensive and absurd regulations; are subject to asset forfeiture without being convicted of a crime; and are subject to selective and arbitrary prosecution for crimes that they may not know about (e.g., an employer who is subject to litigation because of one of his or her employee's sexual harassment of another employee) or are not aware that the activity is a federal crime (e.g., filling in a mosquito-laden swampy area in one's backyard with clean soil).

Why Government Became a Problem Rather than a Solution

Thank heavens we do not get all the government that we are made to pay for.

—Milton Friedman

The United States Constitution and the system of government it created worked well for the first 120 years. It is only in the past 80 years that government grew rapidly both in absolute and relative terms. The Tax Foundation has created a good proxy to show the growth in government, called "tax freedom day," which denotes the number of days that the average American must work each year to pay all federal, state, and local taxes. In recent years, to give an even more complete picture of the cost of government, Americans for Tax Reform has added government spending (which includes borrowing) and the direct cost of regulation to calculate a measure called "cost of government day" (COGD). COGD is the total number of days the average person has to work to pay for all taxes, government borrowing, and regulation. In 1997,

---

[124]from Facts and Figures On Government Finance 1997, published by the Tax Foundation. Additional information on taxes can be found at the Tax Foundation's website at http://www.taxfoundation.org, and from the Americans for Tax Reform website at http://www.atr.org.

Spending Freedom Day was May 12, and the Cost of Government Day was July 3. Here is how it has developed in this century.

Year	Tax Freedom Day
1902	January 31
1925	February 6
1950	April 3
1975	April 27
1997	May 9

In 1902, the US government had been around for 111 years, yet the government burden was still very modest. In the next quarter of a century, the government burden grew by about seven days, ending up about 20% higher relative to GDP than it had been at the beginning of the century. The real explosion in the growth of government occurred in the next quarter of the century, especially between 1930 and 1945, when the burden grew by 48 days, or over 100% in relation to GDP. In the next twenty-five years, between 1950 and 1975, the government burden grew by 24 days, or almost 25% in relation to GDP. Since 1975, the growth in the relative size of government has slowed to a crawl, giving us a government that is about 3% larger relative to the size of the economy than it was 20 years ago. However, as Congress and the Administration have found it more difficult to increase relative spending, they are shifting more of the burden into regulation and mandates on businesses.

When the Great Depression began in 1930, its causes were immediately misdiagnosed; and hence, the economic medicine the economy was given by government made the situation much worse, and resulted in a decade of unnecessary economic misery. Due to the influence of the socialists and Keynesians, there was a belief by those in control that increasing government taxing, spending, and regulation would increase consumer demand and better allocate resources. This increase in consumer demand was supposed to lead us out of the depression to full employment.

A number of economists—most notably the "Austrians" led by von Mises and Hayek, and members of "the Chicago school"—argued from the beginning of the Depression that bigger government was the wrong way to go. Their voices were drowned out by the statist economists, who were in vogue and had their allies in the press. The political class, of course, always wanted more power and greater resources. Keynes and his followers gave the non-socialist politicians the intellectual rationale for a massive expansion of the government sector. Politicians who previously had only a miniscule portion of the people's incomes to play with now could claim that if they were given a third or even half of the income stream to reallocate, their constituents would be better off.

As government got bigger, an obvious slowdown in real growth and new job creation occurred in the US and most of the other industrialized nations. Inflation in the 1970s and early 1980s became the norm rather than the exception. The socialist economies clearly were not working as advertised, and the Keynesians had no answers for the malaise that infected most of the leading economic powers.

Hayek, Friedman, their associates at the Institute for Economic Affairs in London, and their followers did have answers. Their diagnosis and prescriptions began to reach and have influence on a broader audience of opinion leaders in the media and the political world. After Hayek belatedly won his Nobel Prize in 1974, the economic establishment began a decided shift towards free markets. In the last two decades, most Nobel Prize winners in economics have been those who have advocated less rather than more government. Margaret Thatcher, Ronald Reagan, Jack Kemp, and other political leaders who were admirers of the Austrian and Chicago free-market economists were able to explain the ideas to the body politic and to force a change in direction.

The ironic fact is that Bill Clinton, a Democrat, has the pleasure of seeing, on his watch, economic growth without inflation and a balanced budget with full employment. This was achieved with a maximum marginal tax rate that is only slightly over one-half of the maximum tax rate when Ronald Reagan took office (*i.e.*, 39% maximum federal tax rate today versus 70% when President Reagan took office). In 1980, the Keynesian economists and their media fans, almost to a man, were telling the American people and their disciples in the Democratic party that such an outcome was not possible. To repeat, the mantra from the old order in the 1980-1982 period was that it "was impossible" to have full employment, low inflation, a reasonable rate of economic growth *and lower marginal tax rates.*[125]

The intellectual and practical victory of the "supply siders" is still not widely acknowledged by the mainstream media. Members of the media are still in the same sort of denial that characterizes the communist members of the Russian Duma. The theory of cognitive dissonance explains why humans often cannot accept overwhelming new evidence that conflicts with their previously held beliefs.

---

[125]In the spring of 1981, Nobel Prize winning economist Paul Samuelson, Henry Aaron of the Brookings Institution, and I testified before the House Ways and Means Committee of the US Congress, on President Reagan's economic proposals. Samuelson and Aaron (both Keynesians) were opposed to the President's plan, and I spoke in support of it. After several hours of intense debate with members of the committee and among ourselves, we were asked for our summary conclusions. Henry Aaron continued to argue that it was not possible for the plan to work. Paul Samuelson, however, much to his credit, while remaining in opposition to the plan, did concede at the end "that it might possibly work." All of our statements and forecasts are part of the record. The empirical evidence has been in for a long time. Those of us who were supporters of the plan greatly underestimated how rapidly inflation and unemployment would fall, and the extent of the acceleration of economic growth in 1983 and 1984. The opponents, however, not only mis-forecast the amount of improvement, but most were arguing that the plan would lead to higher rates of inflation and unemployment, and lower economic growth—their Keynesian model not only mis-forecast the magnitude of the change, but more importantly, the direction.

This denial of reality, in part, explains why government has only stopped growing significantly as a share of GDP, despite the overwhelming evidence that the US and almost every other country would be better off with a smaller government sector. President Clinton said "the era of big government is over," yet he failed to produce a budget to shrink the government. Even many of the most fiscally conservative Republican members of Congress frequently vote for more spending and more regulation, though they know in the abstract that it is destructive.

They may be aware that the secondary effects are damaging, but few politicians can resist the pressures for more spending from those who get the initial benefit. No one wants to appear heartless. It is also difficult to eschew more regulations as the panacea for the country's ills, especially since those who do are accused of being in the service of special interests. Those fiscal conservatives who think the solution is just electing "better people" are ignoring such pressures in the political marketplace. Until systems are changed to re-establish the checks and balances that worked reasonably effectively for the first 140 years of American constitutional democracy, limited government, as understood by our founding fathers, is unlikely to be restored.

During the Civil War, the US had an income tax for a brief period of time, but it was quickly repealed at the end of the war. The first peacetime income tax was passed by the Congress in 1894. It taxed all income in excess of $4000 at a two percent rate. At the time, only two percent of the population made more than $4000, so ninety-eight percent of the population was tax exempt.[126] Members of Congress from the South and West supported the tax, because they had almost no one in their states making more than $4000. The

---

[126]Charles Adams, For Good and Evil: The Impact of Taxes on the Course of Civilization (New York: Madison Books, 1993), 360.

Southerners believed the Northerners would pay the tax and then tariffs would be reduced, benefiting the South. The Supreme Court quickly ruled the tax unconstitutional, in part because it was arbitrary.

In 1913, the Sixteenth Amendment to the Constitution was passed, which granted the Congress the explicit power to levy an income tax. The first income tax had rates ranging from two to seven percent, with an exemption so large that most people did not pay it. Opponents of the income tax at the time argued that the imposition of such a tax would lead to a slippery slope where rates might go to twenty percent. The opponents were dismissed as alarmists. Thirty years later, the maximum rate reached ninety-one percent.

Income taxes, including the personal income tax, the corporate income tax, and the payroll tax now account for more than ninety percent of all federal tax collections. Without the imposition of the income tax, the government could have never grown so large relative to the economy.

The third reason for the growth in the size of government, in addition to the Keynesian economic rationale and the income tax, is the decline in truth-telling among elected and appointed government officials. Researchers have long known that most people lie about little things (such as "Oh, you have never looked better") because such lies are the oil that keeps a civilized society running. What most Americans disdain are big lies and, in particular, those that can do real damage.

Most professions take sanctions against or at least shun members who deliberately lie about critical data. For instance, a civil engineer who provides false data about the strength of materials he is using in a building project can lose his license and be subject to criminal penalties. An astrophysicist who provides incorrect calculations for launching a satellite will probably have a hard time keeping his job.

In the softer sciences, while it is understood that professionals often will select or interpret data to support their point of view, absolute falsification of data is not acceptable. Recently, two well-known economists were found to have done a very unprofessional job in collecting and interpreting data concerning the employment effects of increases in minimum wages. Their findings seemed to contradict the accepted theory, which holds that unemployment increases among low wage workers and, in particular, teenagers, as minimum wages are increased. Follow-up work by other economists showed that the researchers who had done the earlier study had neither collected nor interpreted the data correctly. While not subject to formal censure, their reputations were severely damaged in the profession, and in the responsible press. (Their false conclusions are still used to promote increased minimum wages.)

However, far less exacting standards of behavior are now demanded of the governing class, even though their falsehoods can be very costly not only in direct monetary terms, but in human lives destroyed. Officials of federal agencies, their supporters in the Congress, and outside vested-interest groups routinely misrepresent the cost effectiveness of government programs the officials oversee. When lawmakers can easily raise huge amounts of money through a compulsory income tax, they are not forced to maintain the type of oversight and show the level of fiscal responsibility that is required by managers in the private sector.[127]

---

[127]The empirical evidence is overwhelming that the current level of government is well above the optimum, which means that, in the aggregate, government programs are not cost effective. A wasteful program may seem like a mere abstraction until one realizes that the tax resources used to support the program make all Americans poorer whereas, if the money were wisely spent, more Americans would be far better off.

The level of dishonest representation by government officials has accelerated as government has grown. There is an almost never-ending demand by some politicians for new federal programs to deal with the problems of hunger, child nutrition, or medical care for the poor. Hundreds of billions of dollars are now spent on dozens of federal programs for these real problems, but the advocates of the new programs rarely ask why the current programs are not working, let alone recommend abolishing them. Over the years, the distinguished labor economist Walter Williams frequently has done calculations of what would happen if you gave every poor person in America a direct payment for his or her pro-rata share of the amount of money the federal government spends on welfare, and the answer is always that they would have a middle-class standard of living. Williams argues that we have not eliminated poverty because many of the programs are grossly inefficient, many in the bureaucratic system have a vested interest in the perpetuation of the problem, and there are some problems that are beyond the ability of governments to solve.

The dishonesty of the people in the political class is not limited to defending the status quo for which they have a vested interest, but equally characterizes their advocacy of new programs in which they have a prospective vested interest. For instance, in the debate about how to curtail smoking, many have suggested greatly increasing tobacco taxes to increase the price of cigarettes to the point where few people would smoke. Many of these same people are claiming that these new taxes will produce hundreds of billions of dollars which can be spent for new government programs. A tax can be raised to the point where there will be very little legal sale of a product (but not illegal, as evidenced by the whole "moonshine" industry of the 1930s-1970s), or a tax can be set at the point where it maximizes revenue, and these two levels of tax are most often quite different. Imagine the level of distress among the trial lawyers and other groups slated to get part of the spoils from the "tobacco settlement," if all Americans were suddenly to decide voluntarily to give up smoking, rather than pay any new tax.[128]

Many of these government officials who have problems with the truth are lawyers. Lawyers should have the highest standards for truth-telling and integrity, but many members of the profession seem to have no reluctance to tell bold-faced lies. This lack of reluctance to lie comes in part because the profession (and in particular the bar associations) seems to condone the most outrageous behavior of their members, including judges.[129]

A major reason Americans have lost their financial privacy, and many other rights, is the lack of faithfulness by judges in their interpretation of the US Constitution. Reasonable people can disagree about many things, including the meaning of some of the words in the Constitution. On the other hand, much of what was written is crystal clear, and the Federalist Papers and other documents provide much supporting evidence for original intent. It is unambiguously clear to most readers (with the exception of some lawyers and judges who appear to have lost their understanding of the English language) of the Fourth and Fifth Amendments, that the degree of intrusion into the private affairs and surveillance of citizens,

---

[128]I was appointed to and served on the federal Quadrennial Social Security Advisory Council (an unpaid position) from 1981-83. We dealt primarily with the problems affecting Medicare. One of the claims that had been made was that smokers were very costly to the Social Security and Medicare programs. Upon examination, the assertion proved to be false, because smokers die earlier and hence have a shorter-term drain on these programs. The biggest drain on these programs are middle-class and wealthy white women, because they live so much longer than other demographic groups. Black males on average collect very little, because of their relatively shorter life spans. These facts—that the programs benefit middle-class and wealthy white women more, while costing males, and black males in particular, more—are not well publicized, because such facts are not politically convenient for the political power structure in Washington.

[129]Many lawyers are very sensitive about "lawyer jokes"—which are by far the most common "profession" joke. The fact which is not funny is that such stereotypes often have a good basis. Most of the problem the legal profession has with its reputation is produced by its failures to discipline its members, and the tendency to run up unnecessary costs.

not to mention property seizures without convictions by federal agencies, would not be approved of by the signers of the document. This is not to argue that the Constitution should never be changed but, if it needs to be changed, it should be done according to the proper procedure, and not by judicial fiat on the whim of some judge.

Of course, many lawyers are well aware of the trend towards limited rights and relative values, and disapprove of them. And there are some courageous ones that are speaking out. Several non-profit legal organizations (such as the Institute for Justice and the Landmark Legal Foundation) have been created to take on the courts in an attempt to restore privacy and property rights. However, too many lawyers remain silent in the face of what they will privately admit is despicable behavior by other lawyers or judges. A code of silence seems to prevail. "Professional courtesy" is valued far more highly than truth, and speaking out against injustice is shunned when it might be considered an affront to a colleague. Many lawyers seem to feel that they are so financially dependent on good relations with the club, that to speak the truth would be economic suicide. The profession will not acquire the respect it craves until more lawyers of courage and conscience demand change. Society needs to have lawyers and judges change their image in order to function as they should. A civil society requires that those who uphold the laws be worthy of respect and honor, and serve the side of justice.

At the beginning of the book, it was noted that there are more than 3000 federal criminal statutes, plus thousands more state and local criminal statutes, plus thousands of regulations for which there are criminal penalties for violations. We are taught that ignorance of the law is no excuse, yet with so many laws everyone is ignorant. The tax law, as had been noted, is so complex that not only can no one individual hope to understand it all, but no reasonable-sized team of tax lawyers and accountants can understand it.

The question is, then, who has a vested interest in the complexity? Economists from even before Adam Smith's time have always been well aware that organized groups (e.g., labor unions, and certain types of businesses), including most professions, seek to obtain monopoly rights from governmental actions that they cannot achieve by competing fairly in the private sector. Quite clearly, lawyers have a conflict of interest when they serve in the Congress and write laws that create work for lawyers. This is true for a member of Congress from any profession, but only with lawyers is the process and practice pervasive. The excessive amount of legally-required paperwork to be done only by lawyers or their employees, for even the simplest of transactions, gives full evidence of the effect. In most modern countries a similar problem has occurred with the growth of the regulatory civil service. Some of these civil servants spend years drawing up new and arcane regulations, only to switch later to consulting, thus multiplying their incomes whilst they advise corporate customers who are at a loss to apply these regulations. Examples abound in areas as diverse as taxation, securities regulation, environmental protection, and air transportation.

Other countries get along perfectly well with a much smaller fraction of lawyers per capita. The legal establishment, seeing the competitive threat from foreign countries, has engaged in an aggressive attempt to export US legal concepts and practices—such as restrictions on financial privacy—to other countries. This attempt has been most blatant in the newly-freed countries in Eastern Europe and the former Soviet Union. Lawyers from US government agencies (including the IRS) and various legal groups have tried to convince many of these countries to adopt a US-style tax system (which is not even appropriate for the US, let alone countries trying to establish viable capitalistic economies). Many of these same lawyers are also strongly advocating measures to severely restrict financial privacy. Some of these countries could learn a great deal from the US legal system that would be constructive—such as the protection of contracts and property rights. The problem is that many of the traveling legal salesmen have been trying to sell the bad of the US system along with the good. They need supervision by good free market economists.[130] In any case, the changes that are coming as a result of the technological change will tend to shake up the profession of the law, as well as the business of banking.

Being an Agent for Constructive Change

In the preceding chapters, much of what is wrong with the US has been detailed. There is much that is right with the US that has not been detailed, deliberately. The purpose of this book is to encourage constructive change, which means to fix what is broken rather than what is not broken. The great beauty of the US system is that constructive changes can still be made.

Some progress has been made. The rate of growth in government has been slowed. Maximum marginal income tax rates are lower than they were two decades ago. Abuses of power by government officials are more widely reported.

The digital age will allow increased numbers of people to escape from government tyranny, and the liberating effects of

---

[130]Many legal scholars have been greatly concerned about the damage caused by economic ignorance among the legal profession and the judiciary. Several University of Chicago scholars, including Richard Epstein, Richard Posner, and Ronald Coase, have been leaders in the move to integrate law and economics. As a result, the distinguished legal scholar and economist, Henry Manne, and others have created "law and economics" programs at several leading US universities, and law and economics programs for judges. If a legal education is deemed necessary to be a judge, a basic understanding of economics also should be a requirement.

the new technologies can be used to constructively exert pressure on elected officials and bureaucrats to move toward liberation. As Woodrow Wilson noted, "Liberty has never come from the government. Liberty has always come from the subjects of government."

The constructive changes that have come about in recent years are a result of the well thought out and active efforts of (often small) groups of individuals. The special interests who seek money and privilege from the government have their lobbyists. Those who seek no favors, but only liberty, need to have their lobbyists. In recent years, many pro-freedom organizations have been established, and a number of them have been effective in changing the political agenda. They need to be supported.

There are a number of measures that the Congress needs to take before digital money becomes the norm. They will only do so if they are pressured by voters and the media. Specifically:

- ◆ Prohibitions on the export of some encryption products need to be eliminated. Such regulations cannot be enforced and they only strengthen the hands of our foreign competitors. Such regulations do not prevent the use of high-grade encryption products by terrorists, drug dealers, or money launderers, but put an inordinate cost upon the law-abiding citizen.
- ◆ Anti-money-laundering laws need to be eliminated. They are a colossal waste of money and almost impossible to enforce, and they greatly interfere with fundamental human rights. The monies used in this quixotic quest could be far better spent on directly

going after the criminals and terrorists. If you believe in tough law-enforcement, you want the money allocated to it to be well spent. Wasting money on trying to enforce laws that are easy to evade, and on trying to prevent activities that are hard to detect, actually helps criminals because fewer resources are devoted to more effective means of crime prevention. Further, the laws tend to be enforced on a very selective basis.[131] Specifically, the Bank Secrecy Act and its amendments ought to be repealed, because it is really a bank anti-secrecy provision that is intrusive, abusive, and not cost-effective or compatible with a free society. The Financial Crimes Enforcement Network agency of the US Treasury should be abolished. Its activities have not been cost-effective, and it engages in very selective enforcement that is not compatible with a free and democratic society.

♦ Laws allowing the forfeiture of assets without a criminal conviction must be repealed. Again, such activities by the government are more characteristic of totalitarian regimes than of free societies. Such laws inherently provide incentives for abuse, and indeed as previously described, are abused on a regular basis.

♦ Taxes on capital need to be repealed. In virtually all cases, they represent multiple

---

[131] As an example, Stephen Kroll, General Counsel of FinCEN, admitted before a seminar at the Cato Institute on December 5, 1997, that, although the donation of campaign funds to Vice President Gore by "Buddhist Nuns" and the passing of funds from Teamsters Union to the Democratic National Committee and back again appeared to be money laundering, no investigation by FinCEN had been undertaken, even though the charges had been public for many months.

levels of taxation, and reduce economic growth because they are equivalent to eating the seed corn of economic development. In addition, in the digital age it will be increasingly difficult and not cost-effective to enforce laws taxing capital.

♦ Government employees should be held to the same standards of professional conduct and liability as are employees and owners in the private sector. The dual standard leads to abusive and arrogant conduct by some government employees, which in turn diminishes respect for all government employees and is unfair to those who are helpful and conscientious.

♦ US law enforcement and regulatory agencies should be prohibited from trying to impose US laws and regulations on an extraterritorial basis. Woodrow Wilson once said, "No nation is fit to sit in judgment upon any other nation." That statement perhaps ought not to apply to totalitarian nations, but it was absolutely correct when applied to democratically-elected regimes that protect the rights of their own citizens. The financial imperialism practiced at times by the US against free-market, democratic nations is offensive and contrary to the American ideals of individual and national sovereignty.

♦ Private businesses, whether they be financial companies, telephone companies, computer software companies, or even legal gambling casinos, should not be required to disclose financial details about the activities of their customers to government authorities (except by court order based on evidence of specific wrongdoing). Governments that fail to make strict distinctions between the functions of business people and those of police officers will tend to become police states. Different types of institutions provide different functions, in order to promote the general welfare of any civilized society. Attempts by government to artificially alter such roles, particularly by requiring private institutions to take on governmental responsibilities, invariably lead to loss of economic efficiency and individual liberty, and a less civil society.

Protecting Yourself

*The only freedom worth the name, is that of pursuing
our own good in our own way.*

–John Stuart Mill

Even though responsible citizens should work for the above-mentioned and other needed changes in law, one would be foolhardy not to take individual action to protect his own assets against corrupt, incompetent, or abusive government officials, and others, in the meantime. Andrew Carnegie is reported to have said, "I put all my eggs in one basket—and watch them." That may have been good advice one hundred years ago, but in the age of arbitrary laws and regulations, and selective law enforcement, it is probably not good advice today.

In the age of digital money, it is easy to acquire financial and real assets in many different countries. For those seeking to have precautionary reserves against the unforeseen, the rule should be to diversify by asset and location. Opening a Swiss or foreign bank account is both easy and legal. It can be done by phone, fax, and over the Internet.[132] A Swiss bank account will give you reasonably good but not perfect privacy protection. It does have the advantage, however, of providing you with a banking system that has the world's record for integrity, competency, and solvency. If you are a criminal, a Swiss bank account will probably not protect you.

Once you have an offshore bank account, you can easily use it to acquire offshore financial and real assets with a high degree of privacy. If you do not currently need income but desire a high degree of financial privacy, acquiring assets from your offshore account (both financial and real) that are likely to result in substantial capital gains may be the best way to go. You are usually only required to report to the IRS income that has been earned, not unrealized capital gains.

There are many types of insurance policies and asset protection trusts, which are offered by institutions in various countries which cannot be seized by creditors or bankruptcy trustees, nor are they reportable to the IRS.

Putting some assets into gold, despite the big drop in price, and other rare assets, can also provide some degree of protection. There are a number of firms that offer both gold bullion and gold coins for sale and will provide depository services. They also offer programs to allow you to borrow against the gold you have purchased so that you are not holding on to a strictly non-earning asset.

As the digital age progresses, it will be increasingly easy for individuals to minimize their cash balances and keep virtually all of their assets in forms that make a positive rate of return.

---

[132]The major Swiss banks now have US offices and websites. People who are interested in more information about a bank can visit its website, or place a call to New York or Zurich headquarters.

As private digital money becomes more widespread, it will be more feasible to make transactions outside the traditional banking system, or at least outside the US banking system, where everything is reported to the government.

Once a person has a reasonable asset base in several countries, it will become easier to move the ownership of these assets from one legal home to another in almost total privacy. Financial service institutions will see the growing market in geographical and asset diversity, as many already have, in addition to increased demands for privacy protection. They will then devise legal and easy-to-use mechanisms to utilize their foreign affiliates to provide the desired privacy and protection. Legal protection for these services will be provided by countries that will see that it is in their economic interest to protect the privacy of foreign asset holders. This process is well underway.[133]

Currently, financial privacy is most often violated by governments and others acquiring information by unencrypted (plaintext) wire and over the air signal taps, as well as by reviewing bank records. As people move to using encrypted messages and jurisdictions with bank privacy, financial privacy will increase. What many will forget, however, is that even though the message is encrypted and the foreign bank is keeping records private, the information also resides in the computer from which the instructions were sent and, unless the computer disc is totally erased or destroyed, confidential financial information can be recovered by unintended recipients.

What the digital age will bring is both a new ease and lower cost in conducting financial transactions anywhere in the

---

[133]Developments in financial privacy and encryption issues can be followed by searching the Internet for sites referring to "encryption" or "financial privacy," and also by reading the relevant books listed in the bibliography and watching for more information written by those authors.

world, with a greatly increased standard of personal privacy, which will not be easily broken by even the most determined governments.

Chapter IX

A TALE OF TWO COUNTRIES: THE YEAR 2013

It was the best of times, it was the worst of times,
it was the age of wisdom, it was the age of foolishness,
it was the epoch of belief, it was the epoch of incredulity,
it was the season of light, it was the season of darkness,
it was the spring of hope, it was the winter of despair,
we had everything before us, we had nothing before us ...

—Charles Dickens

At the end of the millennium, prospects for an enduring world peace had never been better. The few remaining regional conflicts were contained, and posed no significant threat to worldwide stability. For most people, times were good. Fewer people were suffering from hunger and disease, and most countries had embraced democratic capitalism. The world was just entering the digital age. The political leaders of the countries of Freelandia and Malapense, as well as every other country, were struggling to adapt to the changing technology.

Both countries were democratic, capitalistic semi-welfare states in 1999, and were among the ten richest per capita income countries in the world. They had their rich and they had their poor, but most people in both countries considered themselves middle class. Drug abuse and acts of violence were the greatest concerns of the majority of the people in both countries.

In the year 2000, both countries had national elections, and the issues were much the same. In Freelandia, the Constitution party gained control of both the executive and legislative branches of government, while in Malapense the Social Progressive party did the same. The distinctions between the two governments seemed relatively minor at first, but the success of one and the failure of the other drove them in very different directions, with catastrophic consequences for the citizens of Malapense.

By 2013, Freelandia's economy had grown at an average rate of 5% per year, resulting in a more than doubling of its per capita income. Malapense's had grown at an anemic rate of only 1.5% per year, with the result that on average the citizens of Freelandia were now 60% richer than the citizens of Malapense. Freelandia had privatized its social security and national health insurance programs, applied strict cost-benefit criteria to all spending programs and, as a result, had been able to shrink its central government from 21% to only 12% of GDP. Thus, Freelandia had been able to abolish its income tax (and intrusive revenue service), and rely primarily on a low rate consumption tax.

Malapense, on the other hand, increased taxes and the size of its central government, but had less to spend per capita on non-income transfer programs (i.e., social security and national health insurance) than Freelandia, because its economy ended up being so much smaller.

Politicians in both countries had promised to preserve the social safety net, be tougher on criminals, foster economic growth, and not increase taxes.

After appointing a commission to study the likely impact of the digital age on public policies, the ruling party of Freelandia decided that the only course to take in order to preserve their freedom and prosperity was to make radical changes. Their goal became to make Freelandia a prosperous civil society, not a coercive society. Some of the changes that Freelandia made were to:

1. Abolish all tariffs (which were low to begin with) and all barriers to the movement of capital into and out of the country, including reporting requirements on the movement of capital.
2. Abolish all restrictions on the use and export of encryption products.
3. Enact true financial secrecy legislation to protect consumers from the prying eyes (and potential abuses) of any government or other third party.
4. Abolish the right of government to engage in asset forfeiture without a criminal conviction.
5. Eliminate all taxes on capital, including taxes on interest, dividends, and capital gains.
6. Limit the Central Bank to establishing a numeraire for the legal tender money, based on a defined quantity market basket of internationally traded goods and services. All restrictions on the creation of private money-like instruments were abolished, enabling buyers and sellers to contract for payment in any means mutually acceptable.

These measures made Freelandia the most capital friendly country in the world and, as would be expected, huge amounts of foreign capital flooded into the country. The large inflow of capital into the country, coupled with the lack of taxes on capital, reduced the cost of capital, causing a boom in productive investment. The large surge in productive investment caused rapid increases in productivity growth which, in turn, caused rapid and sustained gains in real incomes for most of the citizens of Freelandia.

The new President also established a commission to design a whole new tax and monetary system for the twenty-first century. A far-sighted political economist, who had been a student of the Chicago school of economists, Johann Kempenski, was named as Chairman. The Kempenski commission proposed that the Central Bank be stripped of its bank regulatory powers, and that it be restricted to defining the value of the money (i.e., establishing the numeraire) in terms of a basket (quantity) of goods and services that could be bought with the monetary unit. The basket of goods and services would be restricted to commodities and other items for which there were international liquid markets with a "one world price."[134] Once implemented, all money creation would be done by private financial institutions, and other private companies with balance sheets strong enough to support the creation of any money-like instruments they might wish to issue.

Unfortunately, the new government in Malapense made a crucial error at the beginning of its reign. During its successful election campaign, candidates had promised not to increase taxes, but they had also promised to spend more on government programs desired by some of the special interest groups whose support they needed. They claimed they would obtain the needed revenue by increasing "tax enforcement and compliance." They became nannies with guns.

The Malapense Finance Minister believed they could use

---

[134]Kempenski had personally advocated only using gold, but the other members of the commission convinced him of the merits of going with a broader basket—subject to redefinition—given the accelerating increase of technological change which no one could forecast with certainty.

the new digital technologies to all but eliminate tax evasion. The government required that all payments for goods, services, investments, etc. be made by electronic means and electronic copies of the transactions be sent to the Finance Ministry. (Unlike Freelandia, however, people were not allowed to use smart cards that did not require the transaction to be cleared through a bank—"card to card" systems—or to use those that allowed anonymous spending which functioned like cash.) Both cash and smart card systems allowing financial privacy were prohibited in Malapense, and violators were subject to criminal penalties.

As would be expected, many people began moving their capital to foreign locations that provided bank and financial privacy. The Malapensen government responded by instituting capital controls and capital export taxes. The people responded by importing goods or services and arranging to obtain higher dummy invoices, with the difference being placed in foreign accounts. Others engaged in export of goods and services, underpricing in the official bills and having cooperative foreign buyers deposit the difference in accounts outside of Malapense. Such transactions were easy to arrange because the citizens of Malapense could send encrypted messages to sympathetic and highly cooperative foreign partners, over the Internet or by phone or direct satellite. The government of Malapense then tried to limit the private use of encryption by requiring "back door" means of cracking the encrypted texts. To get around these provisions, the citizens of Malapense turned to using their direct satellite telephones, which connected directly to foreign-owned satellites.

The rulers of Malapense also failed to privatize their social security and national health systems and, as a result, these became increasingly burdensome, eating up greater and greater shares of the budget. The budget problems caused the government to renege on the no-new-tax-increase pledge. The Social Progressives raised marginal tax rates so they could claim that they were only taxing the undeserving rich. These tax increases caused even more capital flight. The demand by people to get their capital out of the country created a new criminal industry specializing in evading the capital controls and high tax rates.

The capital controls and capital taxes caused a dearth in capital investment, and a resulting fall in productivity growth, which in turn reduced the rate of real income growth. High income people and professionals who could easily obtain work elsewhere began to emigrate in greater numbers. The government responded by levying a heavy tax on the assets of people emigrating, which again caused these same people to resort to illegal methods to get more of their assets outside the country.

In their efforts to eliminate all discriminatory and unjust behavior, the government regulators extended their definitions of such legal terms as "sexual harassment" to proscribing detailed rules of appropriate behavior between people. Over time, these rules were extended to children. Enforcement penalties were stepped up to the point where violations of these social codes were treated as felonies, mandating prison sentences.

As the years passed, it became evident that the natural inclination towards protecting the environment was deteriorating. Citizens were no longer concerned about recycling or being careful not to waste natural resources. It seemed as though no one had the time to care about the outside world. Well-meaning environmentalists within the government, despairing of the irresponsibility of the citizenry, picked up the technique of criminalizing all "unacceptable" environmental behavior. No one could be trusted to do anything out of a sense of moral obligation, and therefore the government imposed regulations; it reached the point where one could be charged with a felony for improperly sorting one's trash before setting it out for pickup.

Malapense, like Freelandia, had a strong tradition of free speech. However, the Social Progressives in Malapense decided to make so-called "hate speech," in which religious, ethnic, or racial groups were disparaged, a felony. As the number of regulations and restrictions grew, people began to take out their frustrations by making abusive comments about the government employees, police officials, and lawyers, who were the primary enforcers of the ever growing regulatory state. The government responded by extending the definitions of "hate speech" to cover comments concerning these groups.

The tax code became increasingly complex and arbitrary, so that individuals and businesses never knew if they were in compliance or not. The tax police were given almost unlimited investigatory powers, and the tax courts were becoming nothing more than bureaucratic extensions of the revenue service. Arbitrary enforcement was rife.

The government expanded the use of asset forfeiture, which did not require formal criminal charges to be brought, or convictions to be held, against those who were considered miscreants in some way, or political enemies and, most importantly, as a means of bringing in badly needed wealth to the state's coffers.

The media were cowed by the government. Critics of the government in the press or elsewhere were subject to tax audits, arbitrary tax liens, asset forfeiture, or investigations of possible violations of other laws or rules. Given the number of rules, everyone could be found to have violated some of them. Owners of major media kept their reporters and commentators on a short leash, fearing government reprisals against their enterprises.

To combat crime, which had risen sharply as individuals
became more estranged from society, the government set up
cameras and listening devices in high density areas. As the
cost of these items declined because of rapid advances in
digital technology, the number of cameras and listening devices had greatly expanded to the point where major portions
of the population were under surveillance at any given time.

To combat auto theft, all cars were required to have
monitors installed, which would provide the location of the
vehicle at all times. Clever law enforcement officials recognized in these devices the opportunity to collect all sorts of
information about the performance of the vehicle, such as its
speed, at any place, at any moment in time. The police were
then able to require the installation of computers to monitor
every vehicle everywhere. Traffic tickets were then issued to
owners of vehicles that were "out of compliance."

Digital technology had developed to the point where children were fitted with monitoring devices so their parents
always knew exactly where they were. These devices became
a requirement in Malapense, so that parents could be charged
with neglect if they did not know where their children were at
any given moment. Requirements were soon extended so that
the elderly and disabled were fitted with the devices "for their
own protection." The law enforcement lobby then successfully pushed for making the devices mandatory for anyone
convicted or suspected of having committed a crime. In the
year 2010, the devices had gotten small enough and were
equipped with permanent power supplies, making it possible
to implant them within the human body. The government of
Malapense then tried to make these implants a requirement
for everyone. There was resistance to this effort, so only about
one-third of the population was monitored as of 2013.

By the year 2013, the government of Malapense was able

to know the exact location of one-third of its citizens at every moment, to know the location of each vehicle and whether it was in compliance with all laws at every second, to know the source of all income, and to know exactly down to the last penny how each citizen spent it. The government also had so many laws and regulations, far beyond what anyone could know, that anyone could be charged with some violation at any time. This enabled the government to intimidate the media and the opposition. Everyone understood the unspoken rule: "You speak up, you get charged with a crime."

The majority of the people submitted like sheep. Many did their best to emigrate, even at a terrible financial cost. Finally, there were a sizable number who went into underground opposition, developing devices to thwart the monitors by sending incorrect information. One segment chose to combat the growing authoritarian rule by developing other means of sabotage, including bomb building and biological and chemical warfare. Terrorism, drug use and criminality rapidly increased.

Malapense had turned from a free-market democracy into fascist hell, not through a putsch, but through the old-fashioned corruption of power, aided by new technology. The irony was that most of those elected in the year 2000 had the genuine intent of making their country "fairer" and the citizens safer and more prosperous using the power of digital technology.

Freelandia had taken the opposite course. It had liberated the people to use the new technologies to find new and better ways to improve their own lives. The government did not try to control and regulate. Social vices had fallen sharply, in part because of education programs by churches, private health groups, local communities and many others, for adults and children, but mainly because the majority of people were full of hope, and believed that they had great opportunity to make something of their lives. Perhaps most importantly, they were given the freedom to control their own lives, and they felt a sense of responsibility for themselves and their environment, community, and nation. There was no terrorism (other than an occasional act by an individual suffering from a severe mental problem), because there was little resentment in the society towards the government and other institutions. There were adequate governmental and private safety nets for those who suffered some hardship, because the wealth-creating mechanism of society had not been squelched, and at the same time the majority of society was taught in the public and private schools, as well as in the churches, and had learned that a civil society required the more fortunate to look out for those who had trouble doing for themselves.

Some in Freelandia took advantage of the freedoms and engaged in irresponsible activities but, as in most civil societies, they were a small minority. Their antisocial behaviors were dealt with through local community education and quiet disapproval. For the most part, only the violent and dangerous, or those who had engaged in major property crimes, were imprisoned. The citizens of Freelandia understood that they and their fellow citizens would not be saints all of the time, and that most of them at one time or another would engage in minor transgressions. For these they could be forgiven, because the citizens of Freelandia also knew that most of their fellow citizens, given opportunity and a sense of responsibility, would build a prosperous, non-coercive, tolerant, civil society.

BIBLIOGRAPHY

Adams, Charles. For Good and Evil: The Impact of Taxes on the Course of Civilization. New York: Madison Books, 1993.

Bailey, Norman. Former Special Assistant to the President for National Security Affairs. Interview by the author, 12 December 1997, Washington, DC.

Bandow, Doug. "Clinton's Brand of Jackboot Liberalism." Washington Times 19 October 1997.

Boller, Jörg. "Aus dem Banksafe in den Garten," [From the Bank Safe to the Garden]. Bilanz. Feb. 1997: 80-83.

Boudreaux, Donald J. "Forfeiture Statutes 'An Insult to Society.'" Wall Street Journal, 20 January 1998.

Bovard, James. "Crimes on Paper." American Spectator, January 1998, 44-45.

Browne, F[Frank]. X. and David Cronin. "Payments Technologies, Financial Innovation and Laissez Faire Banking." Cato Journal Vol. 15, No. 1, (Spring/Summer 1995).

Browne, Frank, and David Cronin. "How Technology is Likely to Mould the Future Shape of Banking." The Irish Banking Review. August 1994.

Chydenius, Anders. The National Gain. Translated by Georg Schauman from the Swedish original, published in 1765. Great Britain: Benn, 1931.

Clair, Robert T. "Daylight Overdrafts: Who Really Bears the

Risks?" Governing Banking's Future: Markets vs. Regulation, Catherine England (ed.), Boston: Kluwer Academic Publishers, 1991.

"Clean Getaway for Money Launderers." Journal of Commerce. 10 December 1996.

Coats, Warren and Charles Kelly. "The Simple Analytics of Digital Money: Finance in Cyberspace." International Monetary Fund. Draft Paper. August 1996.

Cowen, Tyler and Randall Krozner. The New Monetary Economics. Cambridge: Blackwell Publishers, 1994.

Dowd, Anne Reilly. "Money Audits the IRS. If the IRS Were a Taxpayer, It Would Owe Big Fines for Misconduct. Instead We All Foot the Bill for More Than $5 Billion." Money Magazine, Vol. 26 No. 1. (Jan. 1997) n. pag. Money Magazine Online.

DuBois, Martin and Douglas Lavin. "American Express, Visa Form Smart-Card Unit." Wall Street Journal, 20 July 1998.

Farah, Douglas. "Moving Mountains of Illicit Cash." Washington Post 9 August 1997.

Friedman, Milton. Capitalism and Freedom. Chicago: University of Chicago Press, 1962.

Garfinkel, Simson. PGP: Pretty Good Privacy. Sebastopol, CA: O'Reilly & Associates, Inc., 1995.

Gates, Bill. The Road Ahead. New York: Viking Penguin, 1995.

Gilder, George. "Fiber Keeps its Promise." Forbes: ASAP, 7 April 1997.

Grabbe, J. Orlin. "The End of Ordinary Money." Liberty, July 1995. Also Online at http://www.aci.net/kalliste/money1.htm

Grabbe, J. Orlin. "The Money Laundromat." Liberty, November 1995.

Hayek, Friedrich. A. Denationalization of Money. 3rd. ed. The Institute of Economic Affairs. Lancing, Sussex: Goron Pro-Print Co Ltd., 1990.

Houlder, Vanessa. "Fear and enterprise on the net," Financial Times, 20 May 1998.

Hyde, Henry. Forfeiting Our Property Rights: Is Your Property Safe From Seizure? Washington, DC: Cato Institute, 1995.

Johnson, Paul. Modern Times. New York: Harper and Row, 1983.

Kinsman, Robert. Your Swiss Bank Book. Homewood, IL: Dow Jones-Irwin, Inc., 1975.

Kondo, Annette. "Nothing Personal: To Avoid Fraud, Guard Identity Data With Care." Chicago Tribune. 20 October 1995. Online. (14 Oct. 1997).

Larson, Ruth. "Senators Pressure Treasury to Fire Inspector General." Washington Times, 11 November 1997.

Lindsey, Lawrence. Address. "Should Money Laundering Be a Crime?" Cato Institute, Washington, DC, 5 December 1997.

Markoff, John. "Clinton Continues to Stumble over the 'E' Word (Encryption)." New York Times, 27 February 1998.

McMenamin, Brigid and Janet Novack. "The White-Collar

Gestapo." Forbes, 1 December 1997, 83-96.

McWilliams, Peter. Ain't Nobody's Business if You Do: The Absurdity of Consensual Crimes in a Free Society. Los Angeles: Prelude Press, 1993.

Melillo, Wendy. "Va. Motorist Gets One Year for Attacking Woman." Washington Post 19 September 1997.

Meyer, Eugene. "Md. Woman Caught in Wrong Net." Washington Post, 15 December 1997.

"Money Fact." Discover. October 1998, 84.

Negroponte, Nicholas. Being Digital. New York: Vintage Books, 1996.

"Privacy on the Internet," Economist, March 7-13, 1998, 19.

Rahn, Richard W. "The New Monetary Universe and its Impact on Taxation." In The Future of Money in the Information Age, ed. James A. Dorn, 81-89. Washington, DC: Cato Institute, 1997.

Reynolds, James E. "Protect Your Privacy: Medical Privacy." Money Online.

Roberts, Paul Craig. "Incoherent Spectacle of Justice." Washington Times, 19 December 1997.

Schneier, Bruce. Applied Cryptography: Protocols, Algorithms, and Source Code in C. New York: John Wiley & Sons, Inc., 1996.

Smith, Adam. The Wealth of Nations. 1776. Reprint. New York: The Modern Library, 1937.

Stansel, Dean and Stephen Moore. "Federal Aid to Dependent Corporations: Clinton and Congress Fail to Eliminate

Business Subsidies." Cato Fact Sheet. (28 Jan 1997): n. pag. Online. (23 Dec. 1997).

Tax Foundation. Facts & Figures On Government Finance. 31st. ed., Washington DC: 1997.

Timmins, Nicholas. "Bungles, Mishaps and Tension Dog FBI." Financial Times, 9 December 1997.

de Tocqueville, Alexis. Democracy in America. Vol. 2. New York: Vintage Press, 1945.

Todd, Walter F. "Banks Are Not Special." Governing Banking's Future: Markets vs. Regulation, Catherine England (ed.), Boston: Kluwer Academic Publishers, 1991.

US Congress. House. Committee on Banking and Financial Services. "Dissenting Views of Ron Paul Regarding Money Laundering Bill," Money Laundering and Financial Crimes Strategy Act of 1998. 105th Cong., 2d. Sess., 1998 H.R. 1756 Rept. 105-608. Internet. Available: ftp://ftp.loc.gov/pub/thomas/cp105/hr608pl.txt

United States. Office of the Comptroller of the Currency of the Department of the Treasury. "Money Laundering: A Banker's Guide to Avoiding Problems." n. pag. Online. Internet. http://www.occ.treas.gov/launderer/orig1.html.

Williams, Daniel. "Leaders are Marching Belarus Stalwartly Into Soviet-Era Past." Washington Post, 12 November 1997.

Wolf, Martin. "Why Banks are Dangerous." Financial Times, 6 January 1998.

Yoder, John. Former Director of the Asset Forfeiture Office at the US Department of Justice. E-mail to the author, 10 March 1998.

INDEX

Discovery Institute
Mission Statement

Discovery Institute's mission is to make a positive vision of the future practical. The Institute discovers and promotes ideas in the common-sense tradition of representative government, the free market and individual liberty. Our mission is promoted through books, reports, legislative testimony, articles, public conferences and debates, plus media coverage and the Institute's own publications and award-winning Internet website (www.discovery.org).

Current projects explore the fields of technology, science and culture, reform of the law, national defense, the environment and the economy, the future of democratic institutions, transportation, religion and public life, foreign affairs and cooperation within the bi-national region of "Cascadia." The efforts of Discovery fellows and staff, headquartered in Seattle, are crucially abetted by the Institute's members, board and sponsors.